CW00350552

Theory and History of Literature
Edited by Wlad Godzich and Jochen Schulte-Sasse

Volume 78. Giorgio Agamben *Language and Death: The Place of Negativity*
Volume 77. Hélène Cixous *Readings: The Poetics of Blanchot, Joyce, Kafka, Kleist, Lispector, Tsvetayeva*
Volume 76. Jean-Luc Nancy *The Inoperative Community*
Volume 75. Rey Chow *Woman and Chinese Modernity: The Politics of Reading between West and East*
Volume 74. Paul J. Thibault *Social Semiotics as Praxis: Text, Social Meaning Making, and Nabokov's Ada*
Volume 73. Hélène Cixous *Reading with Clarice Lispector*
Volume 72. N. S. Trubetzkoy *Writings on Literature*
Volume 71. Neil Larsen *Modernism and Hegemony: A Materialist Critique of Aesthetic Agencies*
Volume 70. Paul Zumthor *Oral Poetry: An Introduction*
Volume 68. Hans Robert Jauss *Question and Answer: Forms of Dialogic Understanding*
Volume 66. Paul de Man *Critical Writings, 1953-1978*
Volume 64. Didier Coste *Narrative as Communication*
Volume 63. Renato Barilli *Rhetoric*
Volume 62. Daniel Cottom *Text and Culture: The Politics of Interpretation*
Volume 61. Theodor W. Adorno *Kierkegaard: Construction of the Aesthetic*
Volume 60. Kristin Ross *The Emergence of Social Space: Rimbaud and the Paris Commune*
Volume 59. Lindsay Waters and Wlad Godzich *Reading de Man Reading*
Volume 58. F. W. J. Schelling *The Philosophy of Art*
Volume 57. Louis Marin *Portrait of the King*
Volume 56. Peter Sloterdijk *Thinker on Stage: Nietzsche's Materialism*
Volume 55. Paul Smith *Discerning the Subject*
Volume 54. Réda Bensmaïa *The Barthes Effect: The Essay as Reflective Text*
Volume 53. Edmond Cros *Theory and Practice of Sociocriticism*
Volume 52. Philippe Lejeune *On Autobiography*
Volume 51. Thierry de Duve *Pictorial Nominalism: On Marcel Duchamp's Passage from Painting to the Readymade*
Volume 50. Luiz Costa Lima *Control of the Imaginary: Reason and Imagination in Modern Times*
Volume 49. Fredric Jameson *The Ideologies of Theory: Essays 1971-1986. Volume 2, Syntax of History*
Volume 48. Fredric Jameson *The Ideologies of Theory: Essays 1971-1986. Volume 1, Situations of Theory*

For other books in the series, see p. 113.

Language and Death:
The Place of Negativity

Giorgio Agamben

Translated by Karen E. Pinkus with Michael Hardt

Theory and History of Literature, Volume 78

MINNESOTA
University of Minnesota Press
Minneapolis • London

Copyright 1991 by the Regents of the University of Minnesota
Originally published as *Il linguaggio e la morte: Un seminario sul luogo della negaivitá*. Copyright 1982 by Giulio Einaudi editore, Turin

All rights reserved. No part of this publication may be reproduced, stored in a retrieval system, or transmitted, in any form or by any means, electronic, mechanical, photocopying, recording, or otherwise, without the prior written permission of the publisher.

Published by the University of Minnesota Press
111 Third Avenue South, Suite 290
Minneapolis, MN 55401-2520
http://www.upress.umn.edu

Printed in the United States of America on acid-free paper

Library of Congress Cataloging-in-Publication Data

Agamben, Giorgio, 1942-
[Linguaggio e la morte. English]
Language and death : the place of negativity / Giorgio Agamben ; translated by Karen E. Pinkus.
p. cm. – (Theory and history of literature ; v. 78)
Includes bibliographical references and index.
ISBN-10: 0-8166-4923-5 (pbk.)
ISBN 13: 978-0-8166-4923-5 (pbk.)
1. Negativity (Philosophy) 2. Language and languages–Philosophy. 3. Death. 4. Hegel, Georg Wilhelm Friedrich, 1770-1831. 5. Heidegger, Martin, 1889-1976. I. Title. II. Series.
B828.25.A4213 1991
111'.5–dc20 90-43185

The University of Minnesota is an equal-opportunity educator and employer.

20 19 18 17 16 10 9 8 7 6

Contents

Preface

The ideas expounded in this book originated during the winter of 1979 and the summer of 1980 in the context of a seminar in which Massimo De Carolis, Giuseppe Russo, Antonella Moscati, and Noemi Plastino participated. The ideas are, in every sense, the fruit of a communal effort. It is nearly impossible, in fact, to translate into writing what was said during the course of a long *sunousia* with "the thing itself." What follows does not constitute a record of the seminar, but simply presents the ideas and materials we discussed in the plausible form that I have organized.

G.A.

Introduction

In a passage from the third conference on the *Nature of Language*, Heidegger writes:

> Die Sterblichen sind jene, die den Tod als Tod erfahren können. Das Tier vermag dies nicht. Das Tier kann aber auch nicht sprechen. Das Wesensverhältnis zwischen Tod und Sprache blitzt auf, ist aber noch ungedacht. Es kann uns jedoch einen Wink geben in die Weise, wie das Wesen der Sprache uns zu sich belangt und so bei sich verhält, für den Fall, dass der Tod mit dem zusammengehört, was uns be-langt.
>
> [Mortals are they who can experience death as death. Animals cannot do so. But animals cannot speak either. The essential relation between death and language flashes up before us, but remains still unthought. It can, however, beckon us toward the way in which the nature of language draws us into its concern, and so relates us to itself, in case death belongs together with what reaches out for us, touches us.] (Heidegger 3, p. 215; English ed., pp. 107-8)

"*The essential relation between death and language flashes up before us, but remains still unthought.*" In the following pages we will thematically investigate this relation. In so doing we are guided by the conviction that we may approach a crucial outer limit in Heidegger's thought—perhaps the very limit about which he told his students, in a seminar conducted in Le Thor during the summer of 1968: "You can see it, I cannot." And yet our investigation is not directly an investigation of Heidegger's thought. Rather, it turns around Heidegger, interrogating this essential relation as it surfaces at certain decisive moments in Western philosophy, particularly in Hegel. At the same time, we will look beyond Heidegger, leaving ourselves open to the possibility that neither death nor language originally belongs to that which draws man into its concern.

In fact, in the tradition of Western philosophy, humans appear as both *mortal* and *speaking*. They possess the "faculty" for language (*zoon logon echon*) and the "faculty" for death (*Fähigkeit des Todes*, in the words of Hegel). This connection is equally essential within Christianity: humans, living beings, are "incessantly consigned to death through Christ" (*aei gar emeis oi zontes eis thanaton paradidometha dia Iesoun*; 2 Cor. 4:11), that is, through the Word. Moreover, it is this faith that moves them to language (*kai emeis Pisteuomen, dio kai laloumen*; 2 Cor. 4:13) and constitutes them as "the trustees of the mysteries of God" (*oikonomous misterion theou*; 1 Cor. 4:1). The "faculty" for language and the "faculty" for death: Can the connection between these two "faculties," always taken for granted in humans and yet never radically questioned, really remain unresolved? And what if humankind were neither *speaking* nor *mortal*, yet continued to die and to speak? What is the connection between these essential determinations? Do they merely express the same thing under two different guises? And what if this connection could never, in effect, take place?

We chose to investigate these problems under the rubric of a seminar on the *place* of negativity. In the course of our research, it became apparent, in fact, that the connection between language and death could not be illuminated without a clarification of the problem of the negative. Both the "faculty" for language and the "faculty" for death, inasmuch as they open for humanity the most proper dwelling place, reveal and disclose this same dwelling place as always already permeated by and founded in negativity. Inasmuch as he is *speaking* and *mortal*, man is, in Hegel's words, the negative being who "is that which he is not and not that which he is" or, according to Heidegger, the "placeholder (*platzhalter*) of nothingness."

The question that gives rise to this research must necessarily assume the form of a question interrogating the place and structure of negativity. Our attempt to respond to this question has led us—through a definition of the field of meanings for the word *being* and of the indicators of the utterance that constitute an integral part of it—to an examination of the problem of Voice and of its "grammar" as a *fundamental* metaphysical problem, and, at the same time, as an originary structure of negativity.

There, with the exposition of the problem of Voice, the seminar reached its end. And yet it might be said, paraphrasing Wittgenstein, that our work demonstrated how little one has accomplished when one has resolved a problem. The path to be followed—if we may properly speak of a path in this case—can only be indicated here. It is not without importance that this path leads toward an ethics—understood as a proper dwelling place that is also liberated from the *informulability* (or *sigetics*) to which Western metaphysics has condemned it. The critique of the ontological tradition in Western philosophy cannot be concluded if it is not, at the same time, a critique of the ethical tradition. Logic and ethics rest on a single negative ground, and they are inseparable on the horizon of metaphysics. And so if truly, as we read in the opening pages of the *Oldest Systematic Program of German Idealism*, in the future all metaphysics must collapse into ethics, the very meaning of this "collapse" remains, for us, the most difficult thing to construe. Perhaps it is precisely such a "collapse" that we have before our eyes; and yet, this collapse has never signified the end of metaphysics, but simply the unveiling and the devastating arrival of its final negative ground at the very heart of *ethos*, humanity's proper dwelling place. This arrival is *nihilism*, beyond which contemporary thought and praxis (or "politics") have not yet ventured. On the contrary, that which thought attempts to categorize as the mystical, or the Groundless, or the *gramma*, is simply a repetition of the fundamental notion of ontotheology. If our demarcation of the place and structure of negativity has hit the mark, then "Groundless" simply means "on negative ground" and this expression names precisely the experience of thought that has always characterized metaphysics.[1] As a reading of the section of Hegel's *Science of Logic* titled "Ground" will amply demonstrate, for metaphysics the foundation is a ground (*Grund*) in the sense that it goes to the ground (*zu Grund geht*) so that being can take place. And as much as being takes place in the nonplace of the foundation (that is, in nothingness), being is the ungrounded (*das Grundlose*).

It will only be evident after following our entire trajectory whether we have succeeded in redefining nihilism and its ungroundedness (or negative ground). Above all, it was important that the structure of this negative foundation—the subject of our seminar—should not simply be replicated in our reflections, but that finally, an attempt might be made to *understand* it.

Note

1. In the context of this seminar, the term metaphysics indicates the tradition of thought that conceives of the self-grounding of being as a negative foundation. Thus the problem of the possibility of a wholly and immediately positive metaphysics (such as that which Antonio Negri attributes to Spinoza in a recent book) remains uncompromised. [See Antonio Negri, *The Savage Anomaly: The Power of Spinoza's Metaphysics and Politics*, trans. Michael Hardt (Minneapolis: University of Minnesota Press, 1991).—Series eds.]

The First Day

At a crucial point in *Sein und Zeit* (sections 50-53), in an attempt to open a passage to the comprehension of Dasein as a totality, Heidegger situates the relationship between Dasein and its death. Traditionally, death is effaced from Dasein and dying is reduced to "an occurrence which reaches Dasein, to be sure, but belongs to nobody in particular" (Heidegger 1, p. 253; English ed., p. 297. The standard English translations of cited texts have been modified by the author and the translators in order to highlight the author's focus in the passages). But here, death, as the end of Dasein, reveals itself as "Dasein's ownmost possibility—non-relational, certain, and as such indefinite, insurmountable" (p. 258; English ed., p. 303).[1] In its very structure Dasein is being-for-the-end, that is, for death. As such, it always exists in some relation to death. "In being towards its death, Dasein is dying factically and indeed constantly, as long as it has not yet come to its demise" (p. 259; English ed., p. 303). Heidegger obviously does not refer here to the death of animals or to a merely biological fact, since the animal, the merely-living (*Nur-lebenden*, p. 240; English ed., p. 284) does not die but simply ceases to live.

Rather, the experience of death in question here takes the form of an "anticipation" of its own possibility, although this possibility boasts no positive factual content. It "gives Dasein nothing to be 'actualized,' nothing which Dasein, as actual, could itself *be*" (p. 262; English ed., p. 307). Instead, it represents the possibility of the impossibility of existence in general, of the disappearance of "every reference to . . . and of all existing." Only in the purely negative register of this being-for-death, when it experiences the most radical impossibility, can

Dasein reach its ownmost proper dwelling place and comprehend itself as a totality.

In the following paragraphs, the anticipation of death, until now merely projected as an ontological possibility, is witnessed even in its most concrete existential possibility in the experiences of the call of conscience and of guilt. However, the opening of this possibility proceeds at a pace with the revelation of a negativity that thoroughly intersects and dominates Dasein. In fact, together with the purely negative structure of the anticipation of death, Dasein's experience of its ownmost authentic possibility coincides with its experience of the most extreme negativity. There is already a negative aspect implicit in the experience of the call (*Ruf*) of conscience, since the conscience, in its calling, rigorously says nothing and "discourses solely and constantly in the mode of keeping silent" (p. 273; English ed., p. 318). It follows that the unveiling of "guilt" in Dasein, which takes place within this silent call, is at the same time a revelation of negativity (*Nichtigkeit*) that originally belongs to the being of Dasein:

> Nevertheless, in the idea of "Guilty!" there lies the character of the "*not.*" If the "Guilty!" is something that can definitely apply to existence, then this raises the ontological problem of clarifying existentially the *character* of this "not" *as a "not"* [*den* Nicht-Charakter *dieses Nicht*]. . . . Hence we define the formally existential idea of the "Guilty!" as "Being-the-basis for a Being which has been defined by a 'not' "—that is to say, as "*Being-the-basis of a negativity*" [*Grundsein für ein durch ein Nicht bestimmtes Sein, das heisst Grundsein einer Nichtigkeit*]. . . . As being, Dasein is something that has been thrown; it has been brought into its "there," but *not* of its own accord. . . . Although it has *not* laid that basis *itself*, it reposes in the weight of it, which is made manifest to it as a burden by Dasein's mood [*Stimmung*]. . . .
>
> In being a basis—that is, in existing as thrown—Dasein constantly lags behind its possibilities. It is never existent *before* its basis, but only *from* it and *as this basis*. Thus "Being-a-basis" means *never* to have power over one's ownmost Being from the ground up. This "*not*" belongs to the existential meaning of "thrownness." It itself, being a basis, *is* a negativity of itself. "Negativity" (*Nichtigkeit*) does not signify anything like not-Being-present-at-hand or not-subsisting; what one has in view here is rather a "not" which is constitutive of this *Being* of Dasein—its thrownness. . . .
>
> In the structure of thrownness, as in that of projection, there lies an essential negativity. This negativity is the basis for the possibility of the negativity of *in*authentic Dasein in its falling (*Verfallen*); and as falling, every inauthentic Dasein factically is. *Care itself, in its very essence, is permeated with negativity through and through* [*durch und durch von Nichtigkeit durchsetzt*]. Thus "care"—Dasein's Being—means, as

> thrown projection, the (negative) Being-the-basis of a negativity. . . . This negativity, moreover, is thus not something that emerges in Dasein occasionally, attaching itself to it as an obscure quality that Dasein might eliminate if it made sufficient progress. (pp. 283-85; English ed., pp. 329-31)

Heidegger begins with this experience of a negativity that is revealed as constitutive of Dasein at the very moment it reaches, in the experience of death, its ownmost possibility. From here he questions the efficacy of the categories within which, throughout the history of Western philosophy, logic and ontology have attempted to think the problem of the ontological origin (*ontologische Ursprung*) of negativity:

> In spite of this, the *ontological meaning of the notness* [*Nichtheit*] of this existential negativity is still obscure. But this holds also for the *ontological essence of the "not" in general*. Ontology and logic, to be sure, have exacted a great deal from the "not," and have thus made its possibilities visible in a piecemeal fashion; but the "not" itself has not been unveiled ontologically. Ontology came across the "not" and made use of it. But is it so obvious that every "not" signifies something negative in the sense of a lack? Is its positivity exhausted by the fact that it constitutes "passing over" something? Why does every dialectic take refuge in negation, without founding it dialectically and without even being able to establish it *as a problem*? Has anyone ever posed the problem of the *ontological source* of negativity [*Nichtheit*], or, *prior to that*, even sought the mere *conditions* on the basis of which the problem of the "not" and its notness and the possibility of that notness can be raised? And how else are these conditions to be found *except by the thematic clarification of the meaning of Being in general?* (pp. 285-86; English ed., pp. 331-32)

Within *Sein und Zeit* these problems seem to remain unanswered. In the conference *Was ist Metaphysik?* (which postdates *Sein und Zeit* by two years) the problem is taken up again, as the investigation of a nothingness (*Nichts*) more originary than the *Not* or logical negation. In this context the question of nothingness is revealed as the metaphysical question par excellence. The Hegelian thesis of an identity between pure being and pure nothingness is reaffirmed in an even more fundamental sense.

At the moment we do not intend to ask whether or not Heidegger provided an adequate answer to the question of the origin of negativity. Rather, within the limits of our research, we return to the problem of negativity, which, in *Sein und Zeit*, is revealed to Dasein in the authentic experience of death. We have already seen that this negativity never outstrips Dasein, although it originally permeates its essence. On the contrary, Dasein encounters negativity most radically at the very moment when, being for death, it accedes to its most certain and unalterable possibility. Hence the question: What is the source of this originary negativity, which seems to be always already invested in Dasein? In paragraph 53, as he delineates the qualities of the authentic experiences of death, Heidegger writes: "In anticipating the indefinite certainty of death, Dasein opens itself to a constant *threat* arising out of its own 'there' " (p. 265; English ed., p. 310). Earlier, Heidegger had written that the isolation that death reveals to Dasein is merely a means of disclosing the *Da* to existence.

If we wish to provide an answer to our question, we must more closely interrogate the very determination of man as Dasein (which constitutes the original foundation of Heidegger's thought in *Sein und Zeit*). In particular, we must concentrate on the precise meaning of the term Dasein.

In paragraph 28, as Heidegger undertakes the thematic analysis of Dasein as Being-in-the-world, the term Dasein is clarified as a Being-the-Da:

> The entity which is essentially constituted by Being-in-the-world *is* itself in every case its "there" (*Da*). According to the familiar signification of the word, the "there" points to a "here" and a "yonder." . . . "Here" and "yonder" are possible only in a "there"—that is to say, only if there is an entity which has made a disclosure of spatiality as the Being of the "there." This entity carries in its ownmost Being the character of not being closed off. In the expression "there" we have in view this essential disclosedness. . . . When we talk in an ontically figurative way of the *lumen naturale* in man, we have in mind nothing other than the existential-ontological structure of this entity, that it *is* in such a way as to be its "there." To say that it is "illuminated" means that *as* Being-in-the-world it is cleared in itself, not through any other entity, but in such a way that it *is* itself the clearing (*Lichtung*). . . . By its very nature [*von Hause aus*], Dasein brings its "there" along with it. If it were to lack its "there," it would not only not exist, but it would not be able to be, in general, the entity of this essence. *Dasein is its disclosedness*. (p. 132; English ed., p. 171)

Again, in a letter to Jean Beaufret dated November 23, 1945, Heidegger reaffirms this essential characteristic of the *Da*. The "key word" Dasein is expounded in this way:

> *Da-sein* is a key word in my thought [*ein Schlüssel Wort meines Denkens*] and because of this, it has also given rise to many grave misunderstandings. For me *Da-sein* does not so much signify here I am, so much as, if I may express myself in what is perhaps impossible French, *être-le-là*. And *le-là* is precisely *Aletheia*: unveiling-disclosure. (Heidegger 4, p. 182)

Thus Dasein signifies Being-the-*Da*. If we accept the now classic translation of Dasein as Being-there, we should nevertheless understand this expression as "Being-the-*there*." If this is true, if being its own *Da* (its own *there*) is what characterizes Dasein (Being-there), this signifies that precisely at the point where the possibility of being *Da*, of being at home in one's own place is actualized, through the expression of death, in the most authentic mode, the *Da* is finally revealed as the source from which a radical and threatening negativity emerges. There is something in the little word *Da* that nullifies and introduces negation into that entity—the human—which has to be its *Da*. *Negativity reaches Dasein from its very Da*. But where does *Da* derive its nullifying power? Can we truly understand the expression Dasein, Being-the-Da, before we have answered this question? Where is *Da*, if one who remains in its clearing (*Lichtung*) is, for that reason, the "placeholder of nothing" (*Platzhalter des Nichts*; Heidegger 5, p. 15)? And how does this negativity, which permeates Dasein from top to bottom, differ from the negativity we find throughout the history of modern philosophy?

In fact, from the beginning of the *Phenomenology of Spirit*, negativity springs forth precisely from the analysis of a particle that is morphologically and semantically connected with *Da:* the demonstrative pronoun *diese* (this). Just as Heidegger's reflection in *Sein und Zeit* begins with Being-the-Da (Dasein), so the Hegelian *Phenomenology of Spirit* begins with sense certainty's attempt at "*Diese*-taking" (das *Diese* nehmen). Perhaps there is an analogy between the experience of death in *Sein und Zeit* that discloses for Being-there the authentic possibility to be its *there*, its *here*, and the Hegelian experience of "This-taking." At the beginning of the *Phenomenology* this construction guarantees that Hegelian discourse will begin from nothingness. Does the fact of having privileged Dasein (this new beginning that Heidegger gave to philosophy—over the medieval *Haecceitas*, not to mention the I of modern subjectivity) also situate itself beyond the Hegelian subject, beyond *Geist* as *das Negative*?

Note

1. [For the term "nonrelational," *unbezügliche*, see *Being and Time*, p. 294, fn. 4.—Trans.]

The Second Day

Eleusis

Ha! sprängen jetzt die Pforten deines Heiligtums von selbst
O Ceres, die du in Eleusis throntest!
Begeistrung trunken fühlt'ich jetzt
Die Schauer deiner Nähe,
Verstände deine Offenbarungen,
Ich deutete der Bilder hohen Sinn, vernähme
Die Hymnen bei der Götter Mahlen,
Die hohen Sprüche ihres Rats.—

Doch deine Hallen sind verstummt, o Göttin!
Geflohen ist der Götter Kreis zurück in den Olymp
Von den geheiligten Altären,
Geflohn von der entweihten Menschheit Grab
Der Unschuld Genius, der her sie zauberte!—
Die Weisheit Deiner Priester schweigt; kein Ton der heil'gen Weihn
Hat sich zu uns gerettet—und vergebens sucht
Des Forschers Neugier mehr als Liebe
Zur Weisheit (sie besitzen die Sucher und
Verachten dich)—um sie zu meistern, graben sie nach Worten,
In die Dein hoher Sinn gepräget wär!
Vergebens! Etwa Staub und Asche nur erhaschten sie,
Worein dein Leben ihnen ewig nimmer wiederkehrt.

Doch unter Moder und Entseeltem auch gefielen sich
Die ewig Toten!—die Genügsamen—Umsonst—es blieb
Kein Zeichen deiner Feste, keines Bildes Spur.
Dem Sohn der Weihe war der hoehn Lehren Fülle
Des unaussprechlichen Gefühles Tiefe viel zu heilig,
Als dass er trockne Zeichen ihrer würdigte.
Schon der Gedanke fasst die Seele nicht,
Die ausser Zeit und Raum in Ahndung der Unendlichkeit
Versunken, sich vergisst, und wieder zum Bewusstsein nun
Erwacht. Wer gar davon zu andern sprechen wollte,
Spräch er mit Engelzungen, fühlt' der Worte Armut.
Ihm graut, das Heilige so klein gedacht,
Durch sie so klein gemacht zu haben, dass die Red'ihm Sünde deucht
Und dass er lebend sich den Mund verschliesst.
Was der Geweihte sich so selbst verbot, verbot ein weises
Gesetz den ärmern Geistern, das nicht kund zu tun,
Was er in heil'ger Nacht gesehn, gehört, gefühlt:
Dass nicht den Bessern selbst auch ihres Unfugs Lärm
In seiner Andacht stört', ihr hohler Wörterkram
Ihn auf das Heil'ge selbst erzürnen machte, dieses nicht
So in den Kot getreten würde, dass man dem
Gedächtnis gar es anvertraute,—dass es nicht
Zum Spielzeug und zur Ware des Sophisten,
Die er obolenweise verkaufte,
Zu des beredten Heuchlers Mantel oder gar
Zur Rute schon des frohen Knaben, und so leer
Am Ende würde, dass es nur im Widerhall
Von fremden Zungen seines Lebens Wurzel hätte.
Es trugen geizig deine Söhne, Göttin,
Nicht deine Ehr'auf Gass' und Markt, verwahrten sie
Im innern Heiligtum der Brust.
Drum lebtest du auf ihrem Mund nicht.
Ihr Leben ehrte dich. In ihren Taten lebst du noch.
Auch diese Nacht vernahm ich, heil'ge Gottheit, Dich,
Dich offenbart oft mir auch deiner Kinder Leben,
Dich ahn'ich oft als Seele ihrer Taten!
Du bist der hohe Sinn, der treue Glauben,
Der, eine Gottheit, wenn auch Alles untergeht, nich wankt.

[Oh! If the doors of your sanctuary should crumble by themselves
O Ceres, you who reigned in Eleusis!
Drunk with enthusiasm, I would

shiver with your nearness,
I would understand your revelations,
I would interpret the lofty meaning of the images, I would hear
the hymns at the gods' banquets,
the lofty maxims of their counsel.

Even your hallways have ceased to echo, Goddess!
The circle of the gods has fled back to Olympus
from the consecrated altars;
fled from the tomb of profaned humanity,
the innocent genius who enchanted them here!—
The wisdom of your priests is silent, not one note of the sacred
initiations preserved for us—and in vain strive
the scholars, their curiosity greater than their love
of wisdom (the seekers possess this love and
they disdain you)—to master it they dig for words,
in which your lofty meaning might be engraved!
In vain! Only dust and ashes do they seize,
where your life returns no more for them.
And yet, even rotting and lifeless they congratulate themselves,
the eternally dead!—easily satisfied—in vain—no sign
remains of your celebration, no trace of an image.
For the son of the initiation the lofty doctrine was too full,
the profundity of the ineffable sentiment was too sacred,
for him to value the desiccated signs.
Now thought does not raise up the spirit,
sunken beyond time and space to purify infinity,
it forgets itself, and now once again its consciousness
is aroused. He who should want to speak about it with others,
would have to speak the language of angels, would have to
experience the poverty of words.
He is horrified of having thought so little of the sacred,
of having made so little of it, that speech seems to him a
sin, and though still alive, he closes his mouth.
That which the initiate prohibits himself, a sage
law also prohibits the poorest souls: to make known
what he had seen, heard, felt during the sacred night:
so that even the best part of his prayers
was not disturbed by the clamor of their disorder,
and the empty chattering did not dispose him toward the sacred,
and this was not dragged in the mud, but was
entrusted to memory—so that it did not become

a plaything or the ware of some sophist,
who would have sold it like an obolus,
or the mantle of an eloquent hypocrite or even
the rod of a joyful youth, or become so empty
at the end, that only in the echo
of foreign tongues would it find its roots.
Your sons, Oh Goddess, miserly with your honor, did not
carry it through the streets and markets, but they cultivated it
in the breast's inner chambers.
And so you did not live on their lips.
Their life honored you. And you live still in their acts.
Even tonight, sacred divinity, I heard you.
Often the life of your children reveals you,
and I introduce you as the soul of their acts!
You are the lofty meaning, the true faith,
which, divine when all else crumbles, does not falter.]
(Hegel 1, pp. 231-33)

This poem, dedicated by the young Hegel to his friend Hölderlin in August, 1796, recounts the Eleusinian mystery, centered, like any mystery, on some ineffable object (*des unaussprechlichen Gefühles Tiefe*). The profundity of this "ineffable sentiment" is sought in vain in words and in "desiccated signs." He who would reveal this object to others must "speak the language of angels," or, rather, experience "the poverty of words." If the initiate attempts this experience, then "speech seems like sin" and "alive, he closes his mouth." A "sage law" prohibits him from carrying "through streets and markets" that which he had "seen, heard, felt during the sacred night" of Eleusis, and finally, this knowledge does not merely live "in the echo of foreign tongues," but rather is "cultivated in the breast's inner chambers."

The fact that the philosopher of the dialectic and *logos* portrays himself here as the guardian of Eleusinian silence and of the ineffable is a circumstance that is often quickly dismissed. This early poetic exercise was evidently composed under the influence of Hölderlin, the poet of the very *Begeisterung* that Hegel had to so emphatically renounce ten years later. For the then twenty-six-year-old philosopher (who, though young, had already read the texts that would most decisively come to influence him, and who was engaged in a frequent philosophical correspondence with Schelling), this poem represents an isolated episode. It is generally supposed that no positive traces of the poem remained in the successive development of his thought.

Obviously, however, such considerations disregard the most elementary hermeneutic correctness, because they fail to examine the fundamental problem—that is, the internal relationship between the Eleusinian mystery and Hegel's thought. Precisely as the ineffable was a vital problem for the young Hegel at a certain point, the way in which he resolved the mystery in the development of his later thought becomes significant and should be the object of a careful study.

Here it is interesting to observe that the Eleusinian mystery appears unexpectedly at another point in Hegel's writing, specifically at the beginning of the first chapter of the *Phenomenology of Spirit* which is titled "*Die sinnliche Gewissheit, oder das Diese und das Meinen*" ("Sense-certainty: or the 'This' and 'Meaning' "). However, the significance of this mystery in the *Phenomenology* appears to be the opposite of that expressed in the poem *Eleusis*, at least at first glance.

In fact, in the first chapter of the *Phenomenology*, Hegel addresses the liquidation of sense-certainty. He carries this out through an analysis of the *This* (*das Diese*) and of indication:

> Because of its concrete content, sense-certainty immediately appears as the *richest* kind of knowledge, indeed a knowledge of infinite wealth . . . Moreover, sense-certainty appears to be the *truest* knowledge; for it has not as yet omitted anything from the object, but has the object before it in its perfect entirety. But, in the event, this very *certainty* proves itself to be the most abstract and poorest *truth*. All that it says about what it knows is just that it *is*; and its truth contains nothing but the sheer *being* of the thing. Consciousness, for its part, is in this certainty only as a pure "I"; or I am in it [*Ich* bin darin] only as a pure "This," and the object similarly only as a pure "This" [*Dieses*]. (Hegel 2, p. 82; English ed., p. 58)

In sense-certainty's attempt to define its own object, it asks, "What is the *This*?" It is then compelled to admit that what seemed like the most concrete truth is a simple universal:

> It is, then, sense-certainty itself that must be asked: "What is the *This*?" If we take the "This" in the twofold shape of its being, as "Now" and as "Here," the dialectic it has in it will receive a form as intelligible as the "This" itself is. To the question: "What is Now?" let us answer, e.g. "Now is Night." In order to test the truth of this sense-certainty a simple experiment will suffice. We write down this truth; a truth cannot lose anything by being written down, any more than it can lose anything through our preserving it. If *now*, *this noon*, we look again at the written truth we shall have to say that it has become empty.
>
> The *Now* that is Night is *preserved*, i.e. it is treated as what it professes to be, as an entity [*Seiendes*]; but it proves itself to be, on the contrary, a nonentity [*Nichtseiendes*]. The *Now* does indeed preserve itself, but as something that is *not* Night; equally, it preserves itself in the face of the Day that it now is, as something that also is not Day, in

> other words, as a *negative* in general. This self-preserving Now is, therefore, not immediate but mediated; for it is determined as a permanent and self-preserving Now *through* the fact that something else, viz. Day and Night, is *not*. As so determined, it is still just as simply Now as before, and in this simplicity is indifferent to what happens in it [*bei ihm herspielt*]; just as little as Night and Day are its being, just as much also is it Day and Night; it is not in the least affected by this its other-being. A simple thing of this kind which *is* through negation, which is neither This nor That, a *not-This*, and is with equal indifference This as well as That—such a thing we call a *universal* [*Allgemeines*]. So it is in fact the universal that is the true [content] of sense-certainty.
>
> It is as a universal too that we *utter* [*sprechen . . . aus*] what the sensuous [content] is. What we say is: "This," i.e. the *universal* This; or, "it is," [*es ist*]; i.e. *Being in general*. Of course, we do not *envisage* [*stellen . . . vor*] the universal This or Being in general, but we *utter* the universal; in other words, we do not strictly say what in this sense-certainty we *mean* [*meinen*] to say. But language, as we see, is the more truthful; in it, we ourselves immediately contradict what we *mean* to say [*unsere Meinung*], and since the universal is the true [content] of sense-certainty and language expresses this true [content] alone, it is just not possible for us ever to say [*sagen*], or express in words, a sensuous being that we *mean* [*meinen*]. (pp. 84-85; English ed., pp. 59-60)

(Let us keep this last paragraph well in mind because in it is already prefigured that resolution of the unspeakable of sense-certainty in language that Hegel proposes in the first chapter of the *Phenomenology*. Any attempt to express sense-certainty signifies, for Hegel, to experience the impossibility of saying what one means. But this is not because of the incapacity of language to pronounce the unspeakable as in *Eleusis* [that is, because of the "poverty of words" and "desiccated signs"], but rather, this is due to the fact that the universal itself is the truth of sense-certainty, and thus it is precisely this truth that language says perfectly.)

In fact, at the very moment sense-certainty attempts to come out of itself and to indicate (*zeigen*) what it means, it must necessarily realize that what it believed it could immediately embrace in the gesture of demonstrating, is, in reality, a process of mediation, or more properly, a true and proper dialectic that, as such, always contains within itself a negation:

> The Now is indicated, *this* Now. "Now"; it has already ceased to be in the act of indicating it. The Now that *is*, is another Now than the one indicated, and we see that the Now is just this: to be no more just when it is. The Now, as it is indicated to us, is Now that *has been* [*gewesenes*], and this is its truth; it has not the truth of *being*. Yet this

> much is true, that it has been. But what *has been* is, in fact, not a being [*was gewesen ist, ist in der Tat kein Wesen*]; *it is not*, and it was with *being* that we were concerned.
>
> In this act of indicating, then, we see merely a movement which takes the following course: (1) I indicate the "Now" and it is asserted to be the truth. I indicate it, however, as something that *has been*, or as something that has been superseded [*Aufgehobenes*]; I set aside the first truth. (2) I now assert as the second truth that it *has been*, that it is superseded. (3) But what has been, *is not*; I set aside the second truth, its *having been*, its supersession, and thereby negate the negations of the "Now," and thus return to the first assertion, that the *"Now" is*. (pp. 88-89; English ed., p. 63)

To demonstrate something, to desire to grasp the *This* in the act of indication (*das Diese nehmen*, Hegel will later say), signifies a realization that sense-certainty is, in actuality, a dialectical process of negation and mediation; the "natural consciousness" (*das natürliche Bewusstsein*) one might wish to place at the beginning as absolute, is, in fact, always already a "history" (p. 90).

It is at this point in the *Phenomenology* that Hegel once again invokes the figure of the Eleusinian mystery, which he had sung ten years earlier in the poem to Hölderlin:

> In this respect we can tell those who assert the truth and certainty of the reality of sense-objects that they should go back to the most elementary school of wisdom, viz. the ancient Eleusinian mysteries of Ceres and Bacchus, and that they have still to learn the mystery of eating bread and drinking wine. For he who is initiated into these mysteries not only comes to doubt [*zum Zweifel*] the being of sensuous things, but to despair [*zur Verzweiflung*] of it; in part he himself accomplishes their negativity, and in part he sees them accomplish it themselves. Even the animals are not shut out from this wisdom but, on the contrary, show themselves to be most profoundly initiated into it; for they do not just stand idly in front of sensuous things as if these possessed intrinsic being, but, despairing of their reality, and completely assured of their negativity, they grasp them without hesitation and consume them. And all Nature, like the animals, celebrates these open mysteries which teach the truth about sensuous things. (p. 91; English ed., p. 65)

What has changed in this experience of the mystery with respect to the poem *Eleusis*? Why does Hegel come back to call into question Eleusinian wisdom? Can we say that here Hegel has simply disavowed the Eleusinian unspeakable, that he has reduced to nothing the very ineffability he had so fervidly upheld in his youthful hymn? Absolutely not. We can even say that the unspeakable here is guarded by language, much more jealously than it was guarded by the silence of the initiate, who disdained the "desiccated signs" and, though still alive, closed his mouth. Those who maintain the primacy of sense-certainty, Hegel writes,

> . . . *mean* "this" bit of paper on which I am writing—or rather have written—"this"; but what they mean is not what they say [*was sie meinen, sagen sie nicht*]. If they actually wanted to *say* "this" bit of paper which they mean, if they wanted to *say* it [*Wenn sie wirklich dieses Stück Papier, das sie meinen, sagen wollten, und die Wollten sagen*], then this is impossible, because the sensuous This that is meant *cannot be reached* by language, which belongs to consciousness, i.e. to that which is inherently universal. In the actual attempt to say it, it would therefore crumble away; those who started to describe it would not be able to complete the description, but would be compelled to leave it to others, who would themselves finally have to admit to speaking about something which *is not*. (pp. 91-92; English ed., p. 66)

That which is thus unspeakable, for language, is none other than the very meaning, the *Meinung*, which, as such, remains necessarily unsaid in every saying: but this un-said, in itself, is simply a negative and a universal, and it is precisely in recognizing it in its truth that language speaks it for what it is and "takes it up in truth":

> But if I want to help out language—which has the divine nature of directly reversing the meaning of what is said, of making it into something else, and thus not letting what is meant *get into words* at all—by *indicating* this bit of paper, experience teaches me what the truth of sense-certainty in fact is: I point it out as a "Here," which is a Here of other Heres, or is in its own self a "simple togetherness of many Heres"; i.e. it is a universal. I take it up then as it is in truth, and instead of knowing something immediate I take the truth of it, or *perceive* it [*nehme ich wahr*]. (p. 92; English ed., p. 66)

The content of the Eleusinian mystery is nothing more than this: experiencing the negativity that is always already inherent in any meaning, in any *Meinung* of sense-certainty. The initiate learns here to not say what he means; but in these terms he has no need to remain silent as in the poem *Eleusis*, or to experience the "poverty of words." Just as the animal preserves the truth of sensuous things simply by devouring them, that is, by recognizing them as nothing, so language guards the unspeakable by speaking it, that is, by grasping it in its negativity. The "sacred law" of the Goddess of Eleusis, who, in the youthful hymn, prohibited the initiate from revealing in words what he had "seen, heard, felt" during the night, is now subsumed by language itself, which has the "divine nature" that prevents *Meinung* from being put into words. The Eleusinian mystery of the *Phenomenology* is thus the same mystery of the poem *Eleusis*; but now language has captured in itself the power of silence, and that which appeared earlier as unspeakable "profundity" can be guarded (in its negative capacity) in the very heart of the word. *Omnis locutio*—we might say, borrowing an axiom from Nicholas of Cusa—*ineffabile fatur*, all speech speaks the ineffable. It speaks it; that is, it demonstrates it for what it is: a *Nichtigkeit*, a nothingness. The true *pietas* toward the unspeakable thus belongs to language and its divine nature, not merely to silence or to the chattering of a natural consciousness that "does not know what it says." Through the reference to the Eleusinian mystery, the *Phenomenology of Spirit* begins with a "truth-taking" (a *Wahrnehmung*) of mystic silence: as Hegel wrote in an important passage from the *Preface*, that should be carefully considered, mystical ecstasy, in its turbidity, "was nothing other than the *pure Notion*" (*der reine Begriff*, p. 66).

(Kojève could thus correctly suggest that "the point of departure for the Hegelian system is analogous to that point in pre–Hegelian systems that leads necessarily to silence [or to contradictory discourse]"; [Kojève 1, p. 18]. The originality of the Hegelian system is that, through the power of the negative, this unspeakable point no longer produces any solution of continuity or any leap into the ineffable. At every point the Notion is at work, at every point in speech blows the negative breath of *Geist*, in every word is spoken the unspeakability of *Meinung*, manifested in its negativity. For this reason, Kojève notes, the point of departure for the Hegelian system is a double point in the sense that it is both a point of departure and a point of arrival, and moreover, it can be shifted, according to the circumstances, to any place in the discourse.)

Thus, the power of the negative that language guards within itself was learned in the "primary schools" of Eleusis. It is possible to "take the *This*" only if one comes to realize that the significance of the *This* is, in reality, a *Not-this* that it contains; that is, an essential negativity. And the "richness of sensuous knowledge," Hegel writes, belongs only to the *Wahrnehmung* that accomplishes this experience fully, since only this truth-taking "has *negation* [hat die *Negation*], difference, and multiplicity in its being" (p. 94). In fact, it is in relation to this *Wahrnehmung* of the *This* that Hegel articulates completely for the first time in the *Phenomenology* the explanation of the dialectical significance of the term *Aufhebung*:

> The This is, therefore, established as *not* This, or as something superseded (*aufgehoben*); and hence not as Nothing, but as a determinate Nothing, the Nothing of a content, viz. of the This. Consequently, the sense-element is still present, but not in the way it was supposed to be in [the position of] immediate certainty: not as the singular item that is "meant," but as a universal, or as that which will be defined as a *property*. *Supersession* [*das Aufheben*] exhibits its true twofold meaning which we have seen in the negative: it is at once a *negating* and a *preserving*. Our Nothing, as the Nothing of the This,

> preserves its immediacy and is itself sensuous, but it is a universal immediacy. (p. 94; English ed., p. 68)

If we now return to the problem that spurred our investigation of the Hegelian text, we might say that the Eleusinian mystery that opens the *Phenomenology* has for its content the experience of a *Nichtigkeit*, a negativity that is revealed as always already inherent in sense-certainty at the moment when it attempts to "take the *This*" (das *Diese* nehmen, p. 93). Similarly, in *Sein und Zeit*, negativity—which always already permeates Dasein—is unveiled for Dasein at the point where, in the experience of that "mystery" that is Being-for-death, it is authentically its *Da* (its *there*). Being-the-*Da*, taking-the-*Diese*: Is the similarity between these two expressions and their common nodal point in negativity merely casual, or does this coincidence hide a common essence that remains to be investigated? What is it in *Da* and in *Diese* that has the power to introduce—to initiate—humanity into negativity? And, above all, what do these two phrases signify? What do Being-the-*there* and taking-the-*This* mean? Our next task is to clarify these terms.

Excursus 1 (between the second and third days)

The problem of indication and the This *is not particular to Hegelian philosophy, nor does it constitute a merely chance beginning to the* Phenomenology, *selected from many indistinct possibilities. Rather it becomes evident from the appearance of this problem at a crucial point in the history of metaphysics—the Aristotelian determination of the* prote ousia*—that in some manner it constitutes the original theme of philosophy. After listing the ten categories, Aristotle distinguishes, as the first and reigning category (*e kuriotata te kai protos kai malista legomene; Categories *2a, 11), the first essence (*prote ousia*) from the second essences (*deuterai ousiai). *While these latter are exemplified by a common noun (*anthropos, ippos*), the* prote ousia *is exemplified by* o tis anthropos, o tis ippos, *this certain man, this certain horse. (The Greek article originally had the value of a demonstrative pronoun, and this persisted even until Homer's time. In order to restore this function to the article, Aristotle accompanies it with the pronoun* tis*; in fact, the Latin translators of the* Categories *render* anthropos *as* homo, *and* o tis anthropos *as* hic homo.*) A short while later, in order to characterize more precisely the significance of the first essence, Aristotle writes that "every [first] essence signifies a this that" (*pasa de ousia dokei tode ti semainein*;* Cat. *3b, 10), since what it indicates is "*atomon . . . kai en arithmo,*" indivisible and one in number.*

While the second essences correspond, then, to the field of meaning of the common noun, the first essence corresponds to the field of meaning of the demonstrative pronoun (at other times, Aristotle even elucidates the first essence with a proper noun, for example, Socrates). The problem of being—the supreme metaphysical problem—emerges from the very beginning as inseparable from the problem of the significance of the demonstrative pronoun, and for this reason it is always already connected with the field of indication. Even the earliest commentators noted that the Aristotelian tode ti *refers explicitly to an act of indication. Thus Ammonius (*Cat. *48, 13-49, 3) writes: "* . . . kai esti men oun to tode tes deixeos semantikon, to de ti tes kata to upokeimenon ousias" *("The 'this' signifies indication, the 'that' essence according to the subject").*

The prote ousia, *inasmuch as it signifies a* tode ti *(that is, both the "this" and the "that"), is the point of enactment for the movement from indication to signification, from showing to saying.* The dimension of meaning of being is thus a dimension-limit of signification, the point at which it passes into indication. *If every category is said necessarily starting from a* prote ousia *(*Cat. *2a, 34-35), then at the limit of the first essence nothing more is said, only indicated. (From this point of view Hegel simply affirms, in the first chapter of the* Phenomenology, *that the limit of language always falls within language; it is always already contained within as a negative.) Thus we should not be surprised if we constantly find this original connection of the problem of being with indication throughout the history of philosophy—not only in Hegel, but also in Heidegger and in Wittgenstein.*

Moreover, we notice several significant analogies between the Aristotelian treatment of the first essence and the Hegelian treatment of the Diese *that opens the* Phenomenology. *Even here we encounter the apparent contradiction (which Hegel addresses) that the most concrete and immediate thing is also the most generic and universal: the* prote ousia *is, in fact, a* tode ti, *indivisible and one in number, but it is also the supreme genus beyond which definition is no longer possible. But there is an even more singular correspondence between the two treatments. Hegel had shown how his attempt to "take-the-*This*" remains necessarily imprisoned in negativity, because the* This *emerges punctually as a* not-This, *as a having-been (*Gewesen*), and "what has been [*Gewesen*] is not a being [*Wesen*]." In a passage from the* Metaphysics *(1036a, 2-8), Aristotle characterizes the first essence in terms that closely recall those cited by Hegel:*

> *But when we come to the concrete thing, e.g.* this *circle, one of the individual circles, whether perceptible or intelligible (I mean by intelligible circles the mathematical, and by perceptible circles those of bronze and wood),—of these there is no definition, but they are known by the aid of intuitive thinking or of perception; and when they pass out of this complete actualization (*entelecheia*) it is not clear whether they exist or not; but they are always stated and recognized by means of the universal formula (*logos*). (English ed.,* The Works of Aristotle, *vol. 8, trans. W. D. Ross., 2nd ed., Oxford, 1928)*

Both the "negative" characteristic ("it is not clear whether they exist or not") and the indefinableness that is here in the first essence as it passes out of complete actualization, and thus necessarily implicates the first essence in temporality and in a past, also become manifest in the expression Aristotle uses in defining the prote ousia*: it is* to ti en einai. *However one translates this singular expression (which the scholastics rendered* quod quid erat esse*), in any case it implies a reference to a past (*en*), a having-been.*

*Medieval commentators had already noted a negativity necessarily inherent in the dimension of the first essence. This was explicated in the context of the Aristotelian affirmation that the first essence cannot be said to be either of a subject or in a subject (*Cat. *2a, 12-13). In a passage from the* Liber de praedicamentis, *Albertus Magnus defines the status of the first essence through a double negation (*per duas negationes*):*

> *Quod autem per negationem diffinitur, cum dicitur quae neque de subiecto dicitur neque in subiecto est, causa est, quia sicut prima est in substando, ita ultima est in essendo. Et ideo in substando per affirmationem affirmantem aliquid quod sibi causa esset substandi, diffiniri non potuit. Nec etiam potuit diffiniri per aliquid quod sibi esset causa de aliquo praedicandi: ultimum enim in ordine essendi, non potest habere aliquid sub se cui essentialiter insit. . . . His ergo de causis sic per duas negationes oportet ipsam diffiniri: quae tamen negationes infinitae non sunt, quia finitae sunt ab his quae in eadem diffinitione ponuntur. (Tractatus II, ii)*
>
> *[Moreover, it is defined through negation since the cause is neither said to be of the subject nor in the subject because just as the first cause is in subsisting the final cause is in being. And therefore in subsisting that which is a cause of itself of subsisting cannot be defined through an affirming affirmation. It cannot be defined through something that is cause of itself, that is through predication. Because the final thing in the order of being cannot have under itself any thing that is in itself. . . . Therefore the definition must involve two negations, which nevertheless are not infinite negations since they are bounded by these limits that are posed in the definition itself.]*

The Aristotelian scission of the ousia *(which, as a first essence, coincides with the pronoun and with the plane of demonstration, and as a second essence with the common noun and with signification) constitutes the original nucleus of a fracture in the plane of language between showing and saying, indication and signification. This fracture traverses the whole history of metaphysics, and without it, the ontological problem itself cannot be formulated. Every ontology (every metaphysics, but also every science that moves, whether consciously or not, in the field of metaphyics) presupposes the difference between indicating and signifying, and is defined, precisely, as situated at the very limit between these two acts.*

The Third Day

Da and *diese* (like *ci* and *questo* in Italian, like *hic* the adverb of place and *hic* the demonstrative pronoun in Latin, and also like *there* and *this* in English) are morphologically and etymologically connected. Both stem from the Greek root *to*, which has the form *pa* in Gothic. From a grammatical point of view, these particles belong to the sphere of the pronoun (more precisely the demonstrative pronoun)—that is, to a grammatical category whose definition is always a point of controversy for theorists of language. In its reflection on the parts of discourse (*mere tes lexeos*, Aristotle, *Poetics* 1456b, 20), Greek grammatical thought only came to isolate the pronoun as an autonomous category at a relatively late stage. Aristotle, considered the inventor of grammar by the Greeks, distinguished only nouns (*onomata*) and verbs (*remata*) and classified all the other remaining words as *sundesmoi*, connectives (*Rhetoric* 1407a, 20). The Stoics were the first to recognize, among the *sundesmoi*, the autonomy of the pronoun (even though they treated it together with the article, which should not surprise us given the originally pronominal character of the Greek article). They defined pronouns as *arthra deiktika* (indicative articulations). In this way, the character of *deixis*, of indication (*demonstratio*, in the Latin) was established for the first time. Expounded in the *Techne grammatike* of Dionysus of Thrace, the first true grammatical treatment of the ancient world, this characterization stood for centuries as the specific, definitive trait of the pronominal category. (We do not know if the definition by the grammarian Tyrannio the Elder, who called pronouns *semeioseis*, refers to this deictic character. The denomination *antonumia*, from which the Latin *pronomen* derives, appears in the grammar of Dionysus of Thrace.)

During the course of its development, the grammatical reflection of the ancient world formed a connection between grammatical concepts in the strict sense and logical concepts. The definitions of certain parts of discourse thus came to be joined with the Aristotelian classification of the *legomena kata medemian sumploken*, that is, with the ten categories. Although the definition of the noun and its division into proper noun (*idios legomenon*) and common noun (*koinos legomenon*) made by Dionysus of Thrace can be traced back to the Aristotelian definition in the *Peri ermeneias*, the examples suggest that it reproduces the Aristotelian definition of *ousia* (''*koinos men oion anthropos, idios de oion Sokrates*'').

(The nexus of grammatical categories and logical categories, which appears here in a well-established form, is not, however, merely accidental, nor can it be easily dissolved. Rather, as the ancient grammarians had already intuited in attributing the origin of grammar to Plato and Aristotle, grammatical and logical categories and grammatical and logical reflections are originally implicated one in the other, and thus they are inseparable. The Heideggerian program of a ''liberation of grammar from logic'' [Heidegger 1, p. 34] is not truly realizable in this sense: it would have to be a ''liberation of language from grammar,'' at the same time that it presupposes a critique of the interpretation of language that is already contained in the most elemental grammatical categories—the concepts of ''articulation'' [*arthron*], ''letter'' [*gramma*], and ''part of speech'' [*meros tou logou*]. These categories are not properly either logical or grammatical, but they make possible every grammar and every logic, and, perhaps, every *episteme* in general.)

A decisive event in this context came with the connection of the pronoun to the sphere of the first substance (*prote ousia*), made by Apollonius Disculus, an Alexandrian grammarian from the second century A.D. This link was furthered by Priscian, the greatest of the Latin grammarians and a professor at Constantinople during the second half of the fifth century. Writing that the pronoun ''*substantiam significat sine aliqua certa qualitate*,'' he exercised a determinate importance for medieval logic and theology that should not be neglected if we wish to understand the privileged status the pronoun has occupied in the history of medieval and modern thought. The noun was seen to correspond with the Aristotelian categories of (second) substance and quality (*poion*)—that is, in terms of Latin grammar, the part of speech that designated *substantiam cum qualitate*, a substance determined in a certain way. The pronoun was situated even farther away than the noun, located, in a certain sense, at the limits of the possibility of language. In fact, it was thought to signify *substantiam sine qualitate*, pure being in itself, before and beyond any qualitative determination.

In this way, the field of meaning of the pronoun came to coincide with that sphere of *pure being* that medieval logic and theology identified in the so-called *transcendentia: ens, unum, aliquid, bonum, verum*. This list (which coincides very nearly with the Aristotelian *pollachos legomena*) includes two pronouns, *aliquid* and *unum*, even if the ancient grammarians disputed their pronominal nature. These words were called "transcendentals" because they cannot be contained in or defined by any higher category. As such they constitute the *maxime scibilia*, that which is always already known and said in any received or named object and beyond which nothing can be predicated or known. Thus, the first of the *transcendentia, ens*, does not signify any determinate object, but rather that which is always already received in every received object and predicated in every predication—in the words of Saint Thomas, "*illud quod primum cadit sub apprehensione, cuius intellectus includitur in omnibus, quaecumque quis apprehendit.*" As for the other *transcendentia*, they are synonymous (*convertuntur*) with *ens*, inasmuch as they accompany (*concomitantur*) every entity without adding anything real to it. Thus, *unum* signifies each of the ten categories indistinctly, inasmuch as, on an equal basis with *ens*, it signifies that which is always already said in every utterance by the very fact of saying it.

The proximity of the pronoun to the sphere of the *transcendentia*—fundamental for the articulation of the greatest theological problems—nevertheless receives, in medieval thought, an essential determination precisely through the development of the concept of *demonstratio*. Returning to the Greek grammarians' notion of *deixis*, the speculative medieval grammars attempted to specify the status of the pronoun with respect to the *transcendentia*. While these terms denote the object as an object in its universality, the pronoun—they claim—indicates, instead, an *indeterminate* essence, a pure being, but one that is *determinable* through the particular enactments known as the *demonstratio* and the *relatio*. In a grammatical text of the thirteenth century we read:

> Pronomen est pars orationis significans per modum substantiae specificabilis per alterum unumquodque. . . . Quicumque hoc pronomen *ego*, vel *tu*, vel *ille*, vel quodcumque aliud audit, aliquid permanens apprehendit, non tamen ut distinctum est vel determinatum nec sub determinata apprehensione, sed ut determinabilis est sive distinguibile sive specificabile per alterum unumquodque, mediante tamen demonstratione vel relatione. (Thurot, p. 172)

> [The pronoun is a part of speech that signifies through its mode of being and is specified through some other thing. . . . Whoever hears these pronouns—I, you, he, or something else—understands something permanent, but what is understood is neither distinct nor determinate nor under determinate understanding; however, it can be determined and distinguished and specified through some other thing, by means of demonstration or relation.]

Demonstration (or, in the case of the relative pronoun, relation) completes and replenishes the meaning of the pronoun, and so it is considered "consubstantial"

(p. 173) with the pronoun. Inasmuch as it contains both a particular mode of signification and an indicative act, the pronoun is that part of speech in which the passage from signifying to demonstrating is enacted: pure being, the *substantia indeterminata* that it signifies and that, as such, is not in itself signifiable or definable, becomes signifiable and determinable through an act of "indication." For this reason, without indicative acts, pronouns—as the medieval grammarians affirm, following Priscian—remain "null and void":

> Pronomina ergo, si carent demonstratione vel relatione, cassa sunt et vana, non quia in sua specie non remanerent, sed quia sine demonstratione et relatione, nihil certum et determinatum supponerent. (Thurot, p. 175)
>
> [Therefore, if pronouns lack demonstration or relation they are null and void, not because they change in appearance but because without demonstration or relation they posit nothing certain and determinate.]

It is within this historical perspective that we can begin to examine the indissoluble link between pronoun (the *This*) an indication that permits Hegel to transform sense-certainty into a dialectical process.

In what does the *demonstratio* that replenishes the significance of the pronoun consist? How is it possible that something like pure being (the *ousia*) can be "indicated"? (Already Aristotle, positing the problem of the *deixis* of the *ousia,* had written: "We will not indicate [the *ousia*, the *ti estin*] with our senses or with a finger." *Posterior Analytics* 92b.)

Medieval logico-grammatical thought (including, for example, the *Grammatica speculativa* of Thomas of Erfurt, which was the basis for Heidegger's *Habilitationschrift* on Duns Scotus) distinguishes two types of *demonstratio*. The first may refer to the senses (*demonstratio ad sensum*), in which case it signifies that which it indicates (thus there will be a connection between signifying and demonstrating: "*hoc quod demonstrat, significat, ut ille currit*"). The second type may refer to the intellect (*demonstratio ad intellectum*), in which case it does not signify that which it indicates, but rather something else ("*hoc quod demonstrat non significat, sed aliud, ut haec herba crescit in horto meo, hic unum demonstratur et aliud significatur*"). According to Thomas of Erfurt, this is also the *modus significandi* of the proper noun: "*ut si dicam demonstrato Joanne, iste fuit Joannes, hic unum demonstratur et aliud in numeros significatur*"). What is the source of this *aliud*, this alterity that is at stake in the *demonstratio ad intellectum*?

The medieval grammarians realized that they were facing two different types of presence, one certain and immediate, and another into which a *temporal difference* had already insinuated itself, and that was, thus, less certain. The passage from demonstration to signification remained problematic, at least in this case. A grammarian from the thirteenth century (Thurot, p. 175), explicitly referring to the union of soul and body, represented the significance of the pronoun as a union of the *modus significandi* of indication (in the pronoun) with the *modus significandi* of the indicated (in the indicated *noun, qui est in nomine demonstrato*). The indication at stake in the pronoun consists in the union of these two modes of signifying; that is, it is a linguistic, not a tangible, fact. The precise nature of this union (if we exclude a few significant references to the *actus loquendi* and to the *prolatio vocis*) remains, nevertheless, just as obscure and indefinite as the nature of the union between body and soul.

In its intuition of the complex nature of indication and its necessary reference to a linguistic dimension, medieval thought became aware of the problematic nature of the passage from *signifying* to *showing*, but does not manage to work it out. It was the task of modern linguistics to take the decisive step in this direction, but this was possible only because modern philosophy, from Descartes to Kant to Husserl, has been primarily a reflection on the status of the pronoun *I*.

Modern linguistics classifies pronouns as *indicators of the utterance* (Benveniste) or *shifters* (Jakobson). In his studies on the nature of pronouns and the formal apparatus of the utterance, Benveniste identifies the essential character of pronouns (along with the other indicators of the utterance, such as ''here,'' ''now,'' ''today,'' and ''tomorrow'') in their relation to the instance of discourse. In fact, it is impossible to find an objective referent for this class of terms, which means that they can be defined only by means of a reference to the instance of discourse that contains them. Benveniste asks:

> What is the ''reality'' to which *I* or *you* refers? Only a ''reality of discourse'' that is something quite singular. *I* can only be defined in terms of ''locutions'' not in objective terms, as is possible for a nominal sign. *I* signifies ''the person who utters the present instance of discourse containing *I*.'' By definition an instance is unique and valid only in its uniqueness. . . . This constant and necessary reference to the instance of discourse constitutes the move that unites I/you with a series of ''indicators'' that, because of their form and their combinatorial possibilities, belong to different classes. Some are pronouns, some adverbs, still others, adverbial locutions. . . . *This* will be the object designated through demonstration that is simultaneous with the present instance of discourse . . . *here* and *now* delimit the spatial and temporal instance that is coextensive and contemporaneous with the present instance of discourse containing *I*. (Benveniste 1, pp. 252-53)

Only through this reference does it make sense to speak of *deixis* and ''indication'':

> There is no point in defining these terms and demonstratives in general through *deixis*, as is the usual practice, if we do not add that *deixis* is contemporaneous with the instance of discourse that bears the indication

> of the person; from this reference the demonstrative derives its unique and particular character, which is the unity of the instance of discourse to which it refers. Thus the essential thing is the relation between the indicator (of a person, a place, a time, a demonstrated object, etc.) and the *present* instance of discourse. In fact, as soon as, through the same expression, this relation of the indicator to the single instance that reveals it is no longer in sight, language looks to a series of distinct terms that correspond symmetrically to the first. These no longer refer to the instance of discourse, but to real objects, times, and "historical" places. Hence the correlatives: I; he; here; there; now; then; today; that same day. (p. 253)

In this perspective, pronouns—like the other indicators but unlike the other linguistic signs referring to a lexical reality—are presented as "empty signs," which become "full" as soon as the speaker assumes them in an instance of discourse. Their scope is to enact "the conversion of language into discourse" and to permit the passage from *langue* to *parole*.

In an essay published a year after Benveniste's study, Jakobson, taking up the French linguist's definition in part, classified pronouns among the "shifters"; that is, among those special grammatical units that are contained in every *code* and that cannot be defined outside of a relation to the *message*. Developing Peirce's distinction between the symbol (linked to the object represented by a conventional rule) and the index (which is located in an existential relation with the object it represents), he defines shifters as a special class of signs reuniting the two functions: the *symbol-indices*:

> As a striking example Burke cites the personal pronoun. *I* means the person uttering *I*. Thus on one hand, the sign *I* cannot represent its object without being associated with the latter "by a conventional rule," and in different codes the same meaning is assigned to different sequences such as *I, ego, ich, ja*, etc. Consequently *I* is a symbol. On the other hand, the sign *I* cannot represent its object without "being in existential relation" with this object: the word *I* designating the utterer is existentially related to his utterance, and hence functions as an index. (Jakobson, p. 132)

Here, as in Benveniste, the function of articulating the passage between signification and indication, between *langue* (code) and *parole* (message), is attributed to the shifters. As symbol-indices, they are capable of replenishing their significance in the code only through the deictic reference to a concrete instance of discourse.

If this is true, what the logico-grammatical reflection of the Middle Ages had only intuited (in the idea of the centrality of the *actus loquentis* and of the *prolatio vocis* for the significance of the pronoun) is here clearly formulated. The proper meaning of pronouns—as shifters and *indicators of the utterance*—is inseparable from a reference to the instance of discourse. The articulation—the shifting—that they effect is not from the nonlinguistic (tangible indication) to the linguistic, but from *langue* to *parole*. *Deixis*, or indication—with which their peculiar character has been identified, from antiquity on—does not simply demonstrate an unnamed object, but above all the very instance of discourse, its taking place. The place indicated by the *demonstratio*, and from which only every other indication is possible, is a place of language. Indication is the category within which language refers to its own taking place.

Let us attempt to define more precisely the field of meaning that is opened in this return to the instance of discourse. Benveniste defines it through the concept of "utterance" (*énoncé*). "The utterance," he writes, "is the putting into action of the *langue* through an individual act of utilization." It should not, however, be confused with the simple act of the *parole*:

> We should pay attention to the specific condition of the utterance: it is the very act of producing an uttered, not the text of the uttered. . . . This act is the work of the speaker who sets *langue* into motion. The relation between the speaker and the *langue* determines the linguistic character of the utterance. (Benveniste 2, p. 80)

The sphere of the utterance thus includes that which, in every speech act, refers exclusively to its taking place, to its instance, independently and prior to what is said and meant in it. Pronouns and the other indicators of the utterance, before they designate real objects, indicate precisely *that language takes place*. In this way, still prior to the world of meanings, they permit the reference to the very *event of language*, the only context in which something can only be signified.

Linguistics defines this dimension as the putting into action of language and the conversion of *langue* into *parole*. But for more than two thousand years, throughout the history of Western philosophy, this dimension has been called *being, ousia*. That which is always already demonstrated in every act of speaking (*anagke gar en to ekastou logo ton tes ousias enuparchein*, *Metaphysics* 1028a, 36-37; "*illud . . . cuius intellectus includitur in omnibus, quaecumque quis apprehendit,*" Thomas Aquinas, *Summa Theologiae,* II, qu. 94, a. 2), that which is always already indicated in speech without being named, is, for philosophy, being. The dimension of meaning of the word "being," whose eternal quest and eternal loss (*aei zetoumenon kai aei aporoumenon, Metaphysics* 1028b, 3) constitute the history of metaphysics, coincides with the taking place of language; metaphysics is that experience of language that, in every speech act, grasps the disclosure of that dimension, and in all speech, experiences above all the "marvel" that language exists. Only because language permits a reference to its own instance through *shifters*, something like being and the world are open to speculation. The transcendence of being and of the world—which medieval logic grasped under the rubric of the *transcendentia* and which Heidegger identifies as the fundamental structure of being-in-the-world—is the transcendence of the event of language with respect to that which, in this event, is said and signified; and the shifters, which indicate the pure *instance* of discourse, constitute (as Kant understood perfectly, attributing transcendental status to the I) the originary linguistic structure of transcendence.

This allows us to understand with greater rigor the sense of that ontological difference that Heidegger rightly claimed as the always forgotten ground of metaphysics. The opening of the *ontological* dimension (being, the world) corresponds to the pure taking place of language as an originary event, while the *ontic* dimension (entities, things) corresponds to that which, in this opening, is said and signified. The transcendence of being with respect to the entity, of the world with respect to the thing, is above all, a transcendence of the event of *langue* with respect to *parole*. And shifters—the little particles *this, here, I, now* through which, in the *Phenomenology of Spirit*, sense-certainty believes it can immediately seize upon its own *Meinung*—are always already included in this transcendence; they always already indicate the place of language.[1]

Note

1. In a different sense from our definition of the linguistic structure of transcendence, J. Lohmann (1948) distinguished the verbal structure of ontological difference in the scission between theme and termination that characterizes *parole* in the Indo-European languages. The difference between the taking place of language (*being*) and that which is said in the instance of discourse (*an entity*) is located in a nearby dimension, but it is more *fundamental* with respect to the difference between theme and termination, inasmuch as it overcomes the plane of simple nouns and reaches the very event of language (that language exists, takes place).

Moreover it is worth noting that the proximity between the pronoun and the sphere of meaning of the verb "to be" probably has an etymological foundation. The Greek pronoun, i.e., **so, *sa,* derives from the root s-, and the verb "to be" (*essere*; es-) could represent a verbalization of this root.

Excursus 2 (between the third and fourth days)

*The link between grammar and theology is so strong in medieval thought that the treatment of the problem of the Supreme Being cannot be understood without reference to grammatical categories. In this sense, despite the occasional polemics of theologians opposed to the application of grammatical methods to sacred scripture (*Donatum non sequimur*), theological thought is also grammatical thought, and the God of the theologians is also the God of the grammarians.*

*This has its greatest effect on the problem regarding the name of God, or, more generally, on what the theologians define as the "translation of the parts of speech to God" (*translatio partium declinabilium in divinam praedicationem*).*

As we have seen, the grammarians suppose that the noun signifies substantiam—cum qualitate, *that is, the essence determined according to a certain quality. What happens—the theologians ask themselves—when a noun must be transferred to designate the divine essence, pure being? And what is the name of God, that is, of he who is his very being (*Deus est suum esse*)?*

In the Regulae theologicae *of Alain de Lille, whenever a noun is used to predicate the divine substance it is transformed into a pronoun (*pronominatur*), and it becomes formless (*fit informe*):*

> *Reg. XVII: Omne nomen, datum ex forma, dictum de forma, cadit a forma.*
>
> *Cum omnem nomen secundum primam institutionem datum sit a proprietate, sive a forma . . . ad significandum divinam formam translatum, cadit a forma, ex qua datum est, et ita quodammodo fit*

informe; pronominatur enim nomen, cum significat divinam usiam; meram enim significat substantiam; et cum videatur significare suam formam, sive qualitatem, non significat quidem, sed divinam formam, et cum dicitur: Deus iustus, vel bonus.

[Rule XVII: Every noun, given by the form, said by the form, falls away from the form.

Since every noun following first institution has been given by property or form . . . when it is translated to signify the divine form, it falls away from the form from which it was given. And thus in some way it becomes formless. A noun is transformed into a pronoun when it signifies the divine. It signifies pure substance and when it seems to signify its own form or quality it does not signify that, but rather signifies divine form, i.e., the just and good God.]

*The noun—referring to the divine substance that is pure substance and "most formal form"—falls away from meaning and ceases to signify (*nihil significat, *in the words of Albertus Magnus), or rather, it is transformed into a pronoun (that is, it passes from signification to indication). Similarly, if the pronoun is used to predicate God, it "falls away from indication":*

Reg. XXXVI: Quotiescumque per pronomen demonstrativum de Deo fit sermo, cadit a demonstratione.

Omnis enim demonstratio est aut ad sensum, aut ad intellectum; Deus autem nec sensu, quia incorporeus, nec intellectu, quia forma caret, comprehendi potest; potius enim quid non sit, quam quid sit intellegimus.

[Rule XXXVI: Whenever a demonstrative pronoun refers to God, it falls away from demonstration.

Every demonstration refers either to the senses or the intellect, but God cannot be comprehended by the senses because he is incorporeal, nor can he be comprehended by the intellect because he lacks form. We have understood more of what is not than of what is.]

Nevertheless, the ostensive function of the pronoun is maintained here through recourse to that particular experience of the word that is faith, conceived as the place of an indication that is neither sensible nor intellectual: "apud Donatum enim demonstratio fit ad intellectum, apud Deum vero demonstratio fit ad fidem."

*It is important to observe that faith is defined here as a particular dimension of meaning, a particular "grammar" of the demonstrative pronoun, whose ostensive realization no longer refers to the senses or the intellect, but to an experience that takes place solely in the instance of discourse as such (*fides ex auditu*).*

Referring to the biblical passage (Exod. 3:13) in which God, urged by Moses to reveal his name, answers, "sic dices eis: qui est misit me ad vos," *the theo-*

logians define the noun qui est, *formed from a pronoun and the verb "to be," as the most congruous and "absolute" name of God. In a decisive passage, Saint Thomas defines the field of meaning of this name as that in which no determinate being is named, but, paraphrasing an expression of Saint John of Damascus, is simply known as "the infinite and indeterminate sea of substance":*

> *Ad quartum dicendum quod alia nomina dicunt esse secundum aliam rationem determinatam; sicut sapiens dicit aliquid esse; sed hoc nomen "qui est" dicit esse absolutum et non determinatum per aliquid additum; et ideo dicit Damascenus, quod non significat quid est Deus, sed significat quoddam pelagus substantiae infinitum, quasi non determinatum. Unde, quando in Deum procedimus per viam remotionis, primo negamus ab eo corporalia; et secundo etiam intellectualia, secundum quod inveniuntur in creaturis, ut bonitas et sapientia; et tunc remanet tantum in intellectu nostro, quia est, et nihil amplius: unde est sicut in quadam confusione. Ad ultimum autem etiam hoc ipsum esse, secundum quod est in creaturis, ad ipso removemus; et tunc remanet in quadam tenebra ignorantiae, secundum quam ignorantiam, quantum ad statum viae pertinet, optime Deo coniungimur, ut dicit Dionysius. Et haec est quaedam caligo, in qua Deus habitare dicitur. (Super I Sent. d.8, q.I, a.I)*
>
> *[In the fourth place, one must say that the other names say being according to some other determination; thus, the word "wise" names some certain being; but this name "who is" says absolute and nondeterminate being by means of some other added specification; hence, Saint John of Damascus says that this does not signify what is God (the "what is" of God), but rather, in some way, the infinite and almost indeterminate sea of substance. Therefore, when we proceed in God by means of the path of negation, we first negate from him the names and the other corporeal attributes; second, we also negate the intellectual attributes, with respect to the mode in which they are found in creatures, such as goodness and wisdom; and so what remains in our intellect is only the fact that God is, and nothing else: and this remains in some confusion. Finally, however, we take away from God also this being itself, insofar as it pertains to creatures and thus remains in the shadows of ignorance; by means of this ignorance, as far as earthly existence is concerned, we unite with God very well, as Dionysus says. And this is that certain shadowy realm said to be inhabited by God.]*

In the final lines of this passage, even the most universal field of meaning for the name qui est *is cast aside. Even the indeterminate being is removed to make room for the pure negativity of "a shadowy realm said to be inhabited by God." The dimension of meaning at stake here goes beyond the vagueness normally attributed to mystical theology (which is on the contrary, a particular but perfectly coherent grammar). In order to understand this, we must take into account the fact that, at this extreme fringe of ontological thought where the taking-place of being is grasped as shadow, Christian theological reflection incorporates Hebrew mystical notions of the* nomen tetragrammaton, *the secret and unpronounceable name of God.* ''Adhuc magis proprium,'' *writes Saint Thomas of this name,* ''est Tetragrammaton, quod est impositum ad significandam ipsam Dei substantiam incommunicabilem.''

> *In Hebrew as in the other Semitic languages, only the consonants were written down, and so the name of God was transcribed in the tetragram IHVH (*yod, he, vav, he*). We do not know the vowels that were used in the pronunciation of this name, because, at least during the last centuries of their existence as a nation, the Israelites were rigorously forbidden to pronounce the name of God. For rituals the name Adonai, or Lord, was used, even before the translation of the Seventy, which always refers to* Kyrios, *the Lord. When the Masoretes introduced vowels into writing during the sixth century, the vowels of the name Adonai were added to the tetragram in place of the original vowels, which were already obscure (and so for Renaissance Hebraicists, the tetragram assumed the form Jehovah, with a softening of the first a).*
>
> *According to an ancient mystical interpretation—already recorded in Meister Eckhart—the four-letter name was identified with the name* qui est *(or* qui sum*):*
>
> *Rursus . . . notandum quod Rabbi Moyses l.I, c.65, hoc verbum tractans: sum qui sum, videtur velle quod ipsum est nomen tetragrammaton, aut proximum illi, quod est sanctum et separatum, quod scribitur et non legitur, et illum solum significat substantiam creatoris nudam et puram.*
>
> *[Once again . . . we should note what Rabbi Moses said regarding this word: I am who I am seems to be what the four-letter name means, or something like that, which is sacred and separate, which is written and not spoken and that thing alone signifies the pure and naked substance of the creator.]*

That which is construed as the supreme mystical experience of being and as the perfect name of God (the ''grammar'' of the verb to be *that is at stake in mystical theology) is the experience of the meaning of the* gramma *itself, of the letter as the negation and exclusion of voice (*nomen innominabile, *''which is written but not read''). As the unnameable name of God, the* gramma *is the final and negative dimension of meaning, no longer an experience of language but language itself, that is, its taking place in the removal of the voice. There is, thus, even a ''grammar'' of the ineffable; or rather, the ineffable is simply the dimension of meaning of the* gramma, *of the letter as the ultimate negative foundation of human discourse.*

The Fourth Day

Dasein, Being-the-*there, das Diese nehmen*, taking-the-*This*. If what we have just said about the meaning of shifters is true, then we ought to reexamine these expressions. In fact, their meaning cannot be understood except through a reference to the instance of discourse. Dasein, *das Diese nehmen* signify: to be the taking place of language, to seize the instance of discourse. For Heidegger, as for Hegel, negativity enters into man because man has to be this taking place, he wants to seize the event of language. The question of the horizon of negativity that we posed must thus be reformulated: What, in the experience of the event of language, throws us into negativity? Where is language located, such that the attempt to grasp its place results in this nullifying power?

But, above all, what does it mean to *indicate* the instance of discourse? How is it possible that discourse takes *place* or is configured, that is, as something that can be indicated? Modern linguistics, which goes so far as to confirm the indexical nature of the shifter, leaves this problem unresolved. Following an ancient grammatical tradition, even linguistics seems to presuppose that, at the limit of the possibility of signification, language can *show* itself, or can *indicate* the present instance of discourse as its own taking place, through shifters. But how does this "indication" come about? In his *Problèmes de Linguistique*, Benveniste bases the indexical nature of the shifter on a "contemporaneity with the instance of discourse that carries the indicator of the person." In this context, Jakobson, following Peirce, speaks about "an existential relation" between shifter and utterance. He writes, "*I* designates the person who utters I." But how is something like indication possible in this case? How can we speak of an "existential relation'' and of a ''contemporaneity'' between the shifter and the instance of discourse? What, in the instance of discourse, permits that it be indicated, permits that before and beyond what is signified in it, it *shows* its own taking place?

A moment's reflection on this question leads us to the conclusion that contemporaneity and existential relations can only be grounded in voice. *The utterance and the instance of discourse are only identifiable as such through the voice that speaks them*, and only by attributing a voice to them can something like a taking place of discourse be demonstrated. As a poet had understood earlier, and perhaps more clearly than the linguists (''I or me are the words associated with voice. They are like the meaning of voice itself; voice considered as a sign,'' P. Valéry, *Cahiers*, I:466), he who utters, the speaker, is above all a voice. The problem of *deixis* is the problem of the voice and its relation to language. An ancient tradition of thought presents this as a fundamental, logical problem —for the Stoics, voice, the *phone*, was the *arche* of the dialectic, and ''*de vocis nemo magis quam philosophi tractant*,'' Servius informs us. Now we must confront this problem.

In truth, at the moment of defining the formal apparatus of the utterance, Benveniste first mentions the ''vocal realization of the tongue.'' But he poses this question only from the point of view of the individual particularities of spoken sounds according to the diversity of intentions and situations in which the utterance is produced. This aspect of the problem, even if it has been ignored by linguists for a long time, has given rise to recent studies (including Fónagy's *La Vive Voix*, on the function of vocal style) that consider the voice as an expression of preverbal (conscious or unconscious) content that otherwise would not find expression in discourse.

It is evident that this way of addressing the problem of voice—though useful—does not interest our present investigation, inasmuch as it merely widens the field of linguistic meaning to include the vocal pronunciation of phonemes, and it does not consider the voice as a pure *indication*—within the structure of shifters—of the instance of discourse. (And yet, the importance of the voice as an expression of affect was already amply recognized by ancient rhetoricians; here it is sufficient to recall the treatment of the voice as a part of the *actio* in Quintilian's *Institutio oratoria* or in the passage from Cicero's *De oratore*, where the voice appears as a *cantus obscurior* present in all discourse.)

The voice at stake in the indication of the shifters is situated, with respect to vocal style, in a different and more original dimension. In fact, as we will see, this constitutes the fundamental ontological dimension. In this sense, the necessary presupposition of the voice in every instance of discourse was already established by late antiquity. Priscian's definition of the pronoun already contains a reference—even if undeveloped—to voice (which at the same time establishes an unexpected relation between voice and the dimension of being, the *sola substan-*

tia): "*solam enim substantiam significant pronomina, quantum est in ipsius prolatione vocis.*" Morever, we know that the medieval logicians and grammarians argued over whether the voice should be included in the Aristotelian list of the categories. Every one of the *legomena*, each of the possibilities for speaking listed by Aristotle, could in fact be considered in itself as pure voice; not simply, however, as a mere sound *(vox inarticulata)* or within a determined field of meaning (*vox* as signifying term), but as the bearer of some unknown meaning. The voice, taken in this way, will then show itself as a pure intention to signify, as pure meaning, in which something is given to be understood before a determinate event of meaning is produced.

An exemplary passage from *De Trinitate* allows us to grasp this dimension of the meaning of voice. Here (X 1.2) Augustine presents, perhaps for the first time in Western culture, the now-familiar idea of a "dead language." Meditating on a dead word (*vocabulum emortuum*), he ponders what would happen if one heard an unfamiliar sign, the sound of a word whose meaning he does not know, for example, the word *temetum* (an archaic word for *vinum*). Certainly, the subject will desire to know the meaning. But for this to happen he has to realize that the sound he heard is not an empty voice (*inanem vocem*), the mere sound of *te-metum*, but meaningful. Otherwise this trisyllabic sound would already be fully understood at the moment it was heard:

> What more can be required for his greater knowledge, if all the letters and all the spaces of sound are already known, unless it shall have become known to him at the same time that it is a sign, and shall have moved him with the desire to know the thing of which it is a sign? Hence, the more the word is known, but not fully known, the more the mind desires to know the rest. For if he knew that it was only a sound, and did not know that it was a sign of something, he would not seek any further, since he had perceived the sensible thing in his consciousness as far as he could. But because he already knew that it was not only a word, but also a sign, he wishes to know it perfectly. But no sign is known perfectly if it is not known of what thing it is a sign. If anyone, therefore, applies himself with ardent diligence to know, and inflamed with this zeal continues this search, can he be said to be without love? What, then, does he love? For certainly something cannot be loved unless it is known. Nor does he love those three syllables that he already knows. But suppose he were to love them for this reason, because he knows that they signify something? (Augustine, English ed., pp. 292-93)

This passage isolates an experience of the word in which it is no longer mere sound (*istas tres syllabas*) and it is not yet meaning, but *the pure intention to signify*. This experience of an unknown word (*verbum incognitum*) in the no-man's-land between sound and signification, is, for Augustine, the amorous experience as a will to knowledge: the intention to signify without a signified corresponds, in fact, not to logical understanding, but to the desire for knowledge ("*qui scire amat incognita, non ipsa incognita, sed ipsum scire amat*"). (Here it is important to note that the place of this experience that reveals the *vox* in its originary purity as meaning [*voler-dire*] is a *dead* word: *temetum*.)

In the eleventh century, medieval logic returned to the Augustinian experience of the unknown voice and conceived it as the basis for the most universal and originary dimension of meaning. In his objection to the ontological argument of Anselm, Gaunilo affirms the possibility of an experience of thought that does not yet signify or refer to a *res*, but dwells in the "voice alone": thought of the voice alone (*cogitatio secundum vocem solam*). Reformulating the Augustinian experiment, Gaunilo proposes a thought that thinks:

> Siquidem cum ita cogitatur, non tam vox ipsa, quae res est utique vera, hoc est litterarum sonus vel syllabarum, quam vocis auditae significatio cogitatur; sed non ita ut ab illo qui novit quid ea soleat significari, a quo scilicet cogitatur secundum rem vel in sola cogitatione veram, verum ut ab eo qui illud non novit et solummodo cogitat secundum animi motum illius auditae vocis effectum significationemque perceptae vocis conantem effingere sibi.
>
> [Not so much the voice itself, which is something somehow true, that is, the sound of the syllables and the letters, so much as the significance of the heard voice; not, however, as it is conceived by he who knows what one usually signifies with that voice (from which it is conceived according to the thing, even if this is true only in thought), but, rather, as it is conceived by he who does not know the meaning and thinks only according to the movement of the soul, which seeks to represent for itself the effect of the heard voice and the significance of the perceived voice.]

No longer the experience of a mere sound, and not yet the experience of meaning, this "thought of the voice alone" opens a new field in thought, which, indicating the pure taking place of an instance of discourse without any determinate accession of meaning, is presented as a sort of "category of categories," always already subject to every verbal uttering. For this reason, it is, therefore, singularly close to the field of meaning of pure being.

In this context we should turn to the thinkers of the eleventh century such as Roscelin. Their thought is not known to us directly, but it was said that they had discovered the "meaning of voice" ("*primus in logica sententiam vocum instituit*," according to Otto of Freising), and they affirmed that universal essences were only *flatus vocis*. *Flatus vocis* is not meant, here, as mere sound, but in the sense of the voice as an intention to signify and as a pure indication that language is taking place. This pure indication is the *sententia vocum*, the meaning of the voice in itself, prior to any categorical significance; in this Roscelin identifies the most universal field of meaning, that of being. The fact that beings, and the *substantiae universales*, are *flatus vocis* does not imply that they are nothing. On the contrary, the field of meaning of being coincides with the experience of the voice as pure indication and pure meaning (*voler-dire*). Restoring Roscelin to his rightful place in this history of modern ontology, we ought now to understand the testimony of John of Salisbury, "*fuerunt et qui voces ipsas genera dicerent*," and that of Anselm, who speaks of "*nostri temporis dialectici . . . qui non nisi flatum vocis putant esse universales substantias*." The "thought of the voice alone," the notion of the "breath of the voice" (in which, perhaps, we ought to note the first appearance of Hegelian *Geist*), is a thinking of what is most universal: *being*. Being is in the voice (*esse in voce*) as an unveiling and demonstration of the taking place of language, as *Spirit*.[1]

If we turn now to the problem of indication, perhaps we can understand how the voice articulates the reference of shifters to the instance of discourse. The voice—which is assumed by the shifters as a taking place of language—is not simply the *phoné*, the mere sonorous flux emitted by the phonic apparatus, just as the *I*, the speaker, is not simply the psychosomatic individual from whom the sound projects. A voice as mere sound (an *animal* voice) could certainly be the index of the individual who emits it, but in no way can it refer to the instance of discourse as such, nor open the sphere of utterance. The voice, the animal *phoné*, is indeed presupposed by the shifters, but as that which must necessarily be removed in order for meaningful discourse to take place. *The taking place of language between the removal of the voice and the event of meaning is the other Voice whose ontological dimension we saw emerging in medieval thought and that, in the metaphysical tradition, constitutes the originary articulation (the* arthron*) of human language*. But inasmuch as this Voice (which we now capitalize to distinguish it from the voice as mere sound) enjoys the status of a *no-longer* (voice) and of a *not-yet* (meaning), it necessarily constitutes a negative dimension. It is *ground*, but in the sense that it goes *to the ground* and disappears in order for being and language to take place. According to a tradition that dominates all Western reflection on language from the ancient grammarians' notion of *gramma* to the phoneme in modern phonology, that which articulates the human voice in language is a pure negativity.

In fact, the Voice discloses the place of language, but in such a way that this place is always already captured in negativity, and above all, always already consigned to temporality. *Inasmuch as it takes place in the Voice (that is, in the nonplace of the voice, in its having-been), language takes place in time. In demonstrating the instance of discourse, the Voice discloses both being and time. It is chronothetic.*

Benveniste had already noted the fact that temporality is produced *in* the utterance and *through* the utterance. He classifies verbal tenses among the indicators of the utterance:

> One might assume that temporality is a structure innate in thought. In reality it is produced in and through the utterance. From the utterance stems the establishment of the category of the present, and from the category of the present is born the category of time. The present is precisely the source of time. It is that presence in the world that only the speech act makes possible, since (if we reflect on this) man has no other way of living "now" at his disposition besides the possibility to realize it through the insertion of discourse in the world. We could demonstrate the central position of the present through an analysis of the tense systems in various languages. The formal present does nothing else but explicate the present inherent in the utterance, which is renewed with each production of discourse, and which, beginning with this present that is continuous and coexistent with our own presence, engraves in consciousness the feeling of a continuity that we call "time"; continuity and temporality that are generated in this incessant present of the utterance, that is the present of being itself, and they are delimited through an internal reference between what will become present and what is no longer present. (Benveniste 2, p. 83)

An excellent analysis, to which we might only add, in order to liberate it from the traces of a psychological vocabulary, that precisely inasmuch as it is generated in the act of utterance (that is, in a Voice and not simply in a voice), the present—as the analysis of the instant throughout the history of philosophy from Aristotle to Hegel demonstrates—is necessarily also marked by negativity. The centrality of the relation between being and presence in the history of Western philosophy is grounded in the fact that temporality and being have a common source in the "incessant present" of the instance of discourse. But—precisely for this reason—presence is not something simple (as Benveniste might lead us to believe), but instead, it guards within itself the secret power of the negative.

The Voice, as the supreme shifter that allows us to grasp the taking place of language, appears thus as the negative ground on which all ontology rests, the originary negativity sustaining every negation. For this reason, the disclosure of the dimension of being is always already threatened by nullity: If, in the words of Aristotle, being is *aei zetoumenon kai aei aporoumenon*, if man necessarily exists "without a way" when he seeks to know the meaning of the word "being" (Plato, *Sophist* 244a), that is because the field of meaning of being is originally disclosed only in the purely negative articulation of a Voice. Moreover, it is this negativity that articulates the split in the field of language between *signification* and *demonstration*, which we saw was constitutive of the originary structure of transcendence.

Now perhaps it becomes clearer why Hegel, at the beginning of the *Phenomenology*, thinks of indication as a dialectical process of negation: that which is removed each time in speaking, *this*, is the voice. And that which is disclosed each time in this removal (through its preservation, as Voice, in writing) is pure being, the *This* as a universal; but this being, inasmuch as it always takes place in a having-been, in a *Gewesen*, is also a pure nothing, and only the one who recognizes it as such without involving himself in the ineffable "takes it in all its truth" in discourse. And now we understand why a nullifying power is inherent in *da* and in *diese*, these little words whose meaning we proposed to examine. "Taking-the-*This*" and "Being-the-*there*" *are possible only through the experience of the Voice, that is, the experience of the taking place of language in the removal of the voice.*

If our analysis is correct so far, we ought to be able to find in both Hegel and Heidegger a notion of the Voice as the originary negative articulation. In the following days we will initiate this task.

Note

1. Even Abelard, who was Roscelin's disciple, distinguishes the voice as physical *subiectum* (the air being hit) from the *tenor aëris*, its pure signifying articulation that (following Priscian) he also terms *spiritus*.

Excursus 3 (between the fourth and fifth days)

With the isolation of the field that we indicated by the term Voice, philosophy responds to a question that, referring to its implicit formulation in the Aristotelian Peri ermeneeias, *might be posed as follows: What is in the voice? What are* ta en te phone? *Aristotle outlines the process of signification in human discourse:*

> *That which is in the voice (*ta en te phone*) contains the symbols of mental experience, and written words are the symbols of that which is in the voice. Just as all men do not have the same writing (*grammata*), so all men do not have the same voices (*phonai*), but the mental experiences, which these directly symbolize, are the same for all, as also are those things of which our experiences (*pragmata*) are the images. (*De interpretatione *16a, 3-7; English ed.,* The Works of Aristotle, *trans. E. M. Edghill [Oxford, 1971])*

*If the meaningful nature of language is explained as a process of interpretation (*ermeneia*), which takes place in this passage between three interconnected terms (that which is in the voice interprets and signifies the mental experience that, in turn, corresponds to the* pragmata*), then what remains problematic is precisely the status of the* grammata. *Why does Aristotle introduce this "fourth interpreter," which seems to exhaust the order of signification? The ancient commentators had already realized that once significance was construed as a reference between voices and mental experiences, and between mental experiences and things, it was then necessary to introduce a fourth element to assure the interpretation of the voices themselves. The* gramma *is this fourth interpreter.*

However, since, as a final interpreter, the gramma *is the ground that sustains the entire circle of signification, it must necessarily enjoy a privileged status within this circle. Greek grammatical thought came to locate this particular status of the* gramma, *in that it is not simply (like the other three elements) a sign, but also an element of voice (*stoicheion tes phonés*). Following what was in a certain sense already implicit in the Aristotelian formula (*ta en te phoné, *that which is in the voice, and not simply the voice itself), the ancient grammarians defined the* gramma *as* phoné enarthros ameres, pars minima vocis articulatae; *that is, as the quantum of the signifying voice.* As a sign, and, at the same time, a constitutive element of the voice, the *gramma* comes thus to assume the paradoxical status of an index of itself (index sui).

This means that, from the beginning, Western reflections on language locate the gramma *and not the voice in the originary place. In fact, as a sign the* gramma *presupposes both the voice and its removal, but as an element, it has the structure of a purely negative self-affection, of a trace of itself. Philosophy responds to the question, "What is in the voice?" as follows: Nothing is in the voice, the voice is the place of the negative, it is Voice—that is, pure temporality. But this negativity is* gramma, *that is, the* arthron *that articulates voice and language and thus discloses being and meaning.*

From this point of view it is possible to measure the acuteness of Derrida's critique of the metaphysical tradition and also the distance that remains to be covered. Although we must certainly honor Derrida as the thinker who has identified with the greatest rigor—developing Lévinas's concept of the trace and Heidegger's concept of difference—the original status of the gramma *and of meaning in our culture, it is also true that he believed he had opened a way to surpassing metaphysics, while in truth he merely brought the fundamental problem of metaphysics to light. For metaphysics is not simply the primacy of the voice over the* gramma. *If metaphysics is that reflection that places the voice as origin, it is also true that this voice is, from the beginning, conceived as removed, as Voice. To identify the horizon of metaphysics simply in that supremacy of the* phone *and then to believe in one's power to overcome this horizon through the* gramma, *is to conceive of metaphysics without its coexistent negativity. Metaphysics is always already grammatology and this is* fundamentology *in the sense that the* gramma *(or the Voice) functions as the negative ontological foundation.*

A decisive critique of metaphysics would necessarily involve a confrontation with Hegel's notion of the Absolute and with Heidegger's Ereignis. *Given that, isn't it precisely the self-withdrawal of the origin (its structure as trace—that is, as negative and temporal) that should be thought (absolved) in the Absolute (that is only at the end, as a result, that which truly is—the turning in on itself of the trace) and in the* Ereignis *(in which difference as such comes into thought; no longer simply the forgetting of being, but the forgetting and the self-withdrawal of being in itself)? Perhaps the identification of the structure of the trace of the origin as a fundamental problem is, however, even older, and is already formed in the* to ichnos tou amorphon morphe *of* Enneads *VI 7.33 (form, the principle of presence as a trace*—ichnos—*of a formlessness). Perhaps it is already in the Platonic* epekeina tes ousias, *that is, in the situating of the idea of good beyond being (*Republic *509b, 9), and also in the Aristotelian* to ti en einai *(being that has always already existed).*

Even Lévinas's critique of ontology, which found its most complete expression in a revision of the Platonic and Neoplatonic epekeina tes ousias *(Lévinas 1978), really only brings to light the* fundamental *negative structure of metaphysics, attempting to think the immemorial having-been beyond all being and presence, the* ille *that is before every* I *and every* this, *the* saying *that is beyond every* said. *(However, the accent Lévinas placed on ethics was not treated in the context of this seminar.)*

The Fifth Day

There is a Hegelian text in which the problem of voice surfaces thematically in such a way as to throw a singular light onto the very articulation of the concept of negativity in his thought—the manuscript of the lessons the young Hegel held at Jena during the years 1803–4 and 1805–6, published respectively for the first time by Hoffmeister in 1932 as *Jenenser Realphilosophie I* and in 1931 as *Jenenser Realphilosophie II.*[1]

Where the previous lessons had followed the "going to pieces" of the spirit and its "concealedness" in nature, Hegel now describes its reemergence into light in the figure of consciousness and its realization though the "powers" of memory and language. In the senses and in imagination, consciousness has not yet come out into the light, it is still immersed in its "night." Hegel writes that the imagination is a "dream, a working-dream or a sleeping-dream, empty and lacking in truth"; and, in a passage from the 1805–6 lessons, this night is described in terrifying terms:

> Der Mensch ist diese Nacht, dies leere Nichts, das alles in ihrer Einfachheit enthält, ein Reichtum unendlich vieler Vorstellungen, Bilder. . . . In phantasmagorischen Vorstellungen ist es ringsum Nacht; hier schiesst dann ein blutig[er] Kopf, dort ein[e] andere weisse Gestalt plötzlich hervor und verschwinden ebenso. Diese Nacht erblickt man, wenn man dem Menschen ins Auge blickt—in eine Nacht hinein, die furchtbar wird; es hängt die Nacht der Welt hier einem entgegen.
>
> [Man is this night, this pure nothing that contains everything in its

simplicity, a realm endlessly rich in representations and images. . . . In phantasmagoric representations he is surrounded by night; suddenly a bloody head juts forth here, there another white figure, and just as suddenly they disappear. One glimpses this night when one looks into the eyes of another human—into a night, which becomes frightening; here each of us is suspended confronting the night of the world.] (Hegel 4, pp. 180-81)

With the sign and its ''mute indication,'' consciousness strips away that which it had intuited in its indistinct cohesion and places it in relation to something else; but the sign is still a natural thing that contains no absolute significance in itself. It is merely placed arbitrarily by the subject in relation to some object. Thus the sign must be abolished as something real so that the dimension of meaning and of consciousness may emerge in its truth: ''the idea of this existence of consciousness is *memory*, and its proper existence is language'' (Hegel 5, p. 211).

Das Gedächtnis, die Mnemosyne der Alten, ist seiner wahren Bedeutung nach nicht dieses, dass Anschauung oder was es sei, die Produkte des Gedächtnisses selbst in dem allgemeinen Elemente seien und aus ihm hervorgerufen, es auf eine formale Weise, die den Inhalt nichts angeht, besondert werde; sondern dass es das, was wir sinnliche Anschauung genannt haben, zur Gedächtnis-Sache, zu einem Gedachten macht. . . . Hierin erhält das Bewusstsein erst eine Realität, dass an dem nur in Raum und Zeit Idealen, d.h. das Anderssein ausser sich Habenden diese Beziehung nach aussen vernichtet und es für sich selbst ideell gesetzt werde, dass es zu einem Namen werde. Im Namen ist sein empirisches Sein, dass es ein Konkretes in sich Mannigfaltiges und Lebendes und Seiendes ist, aufgehoben, es zu einem schlecthin in sich einfachen Ideellen gemacht. Der erste Akt, wodurch Adam Seine herrschaft über die Tiere konstituiert hat, ist, dass er ihnen Namen gab, d.h. sie als Seiende vernichtete und sie zu für sich Ideellen machte. Das Zeichen war in der worhergehenden Potenz als Zeichen ein Name, der für sich noch etwas Anderes als ein Name ist, selbst ein Ding; und das Bezeichnete hatte sein Zeichen ausser ihm; est war nicht gesetzt als ein Aufgehobenes. Ebenso hat das Zeichen nicht an ihm selbst seine Bedeutung, sondern nur in dem Subjekte; man musste noch besonders wissen, was es damit meine. Der Name aber ist an sich, bleibend, ohne das Ding und das Subjekt. Im Namen ist die fürsich seiende Realität das Zeichens vernichtet.

Der Name existiert als Sprache,—sie ist der existierende Begriff des Bewusstseins,—die sich also nicht fixiert, ebenso unmittelbar aufhört, als sie ist; sie existiert im Elemente der Luft.

[Memory, the Mnemosyne of the ancients, according to its true significance does not consist in this: that intuition or whatever it might be, the products of memory itself are in the universal element and are called outside of it; that is, that memory is particularized in a formal mode that does not reach the level of content. Rather, even though memory sets into motion a *fact-of-memory*, something recalled, that is, what we have defined as sensory intuition ("I remember—*ich er-innere mich*"—Hegel will say in the lessons of 1805–6—signifies "I penetrate inside myself, I remember myself—*gehe innerhalb meiner*"). . . . Thus consciousness acquires a reality for the first time, that is, with the condition that it exists in the ideal object only in space and time. That is, in having its being-other outside of itself, this relation toward the exterior is negated and this being-other is placed ideally for itself, such that it becomes a *name*. In the *name* its empirical being is removed from it, that is, it is no longer concrete, no longer a multiplicity in itself, no longer a living entity. Instead it is transformed into a pure and simple ideal. Adam's first mediating action in establishing his dominion over the animals consisted in his granting them names; thus he denied them as independent beings and he transformed them into ideals. The sign, in its preceding power, was as the sign of a *name*. However, this name in itself was still something other than a name, that is, a thing. And the object indicated with the name had its sign outside of itself; it was not posited as something removed. Thus even the sign does not have meaning in itself, but only in the subject; one still needed to know in particular what was meant by it. On the other hand, the name in itself is durable, independent of the thing and of the subject. In the name, the reality for itself existing in the sign is cancelled.

The name exists as a language—this is the existing concept of consciousness—that is not fixed, and so it ceases just as quickly as it comes to be; it exists in the element of air.] (Hegel 5, pp. 211-12)

The name—inasmuch as it "exists in the air" as a negation and a memory of the named object—thus abolishes that which was still natural in the sign, a reality that is other than its own meaning. Shaking the spirit from its sleep, and restoring it to its airy element, the name transforms the realm of images into a "realm of names" ("The waking of the spirit is the *realm of names*," Hegel 4, p. 184). But how was memory able to become language, and thus grant existence to consciousness? It is at this point that the theme of the voice appears in its centrality:

Die leere Stimme des Tiers erhält eine unendlich in sich bestimmte Bedeutung. Das rein Tönende der Stimme, das Vokale, unterscheidet selbst sich, indem das Organ der Stimme seine Gliederung als seine solche in ihren Unterschieden zeigt. Dieses rein Tönende wird durch dies stummen [Mitlaute] unterbrochen, has eigentlich Hemmende des blossen Tönens, wodurch vorzüglich jeder Ton für sich eine Bedeutung hat, da die Unterschiede des blossen Tönens im Gesange nicht für sich bestimmte Unterschiede sind, sondern sich erst durch den

> vorhergehenden und folgenden Ton bestimmen. Die als tönend gegliederte Sprache ist Stimme des Bewusstseins darin, dass jeder Ton Bedeutung hat, d.h. dass in ihm ein Name existiert, die Idealität eines existierenden Dings, das unmittelbare Nicht-Existieren desselben.
>
> [The empty voice of the animal acquires a meaning that is infinitely determinate in itself. The pure sound of the voice, the vowel, is differentiated since the organ of the voice presents its articulation as a particular articulation with its differences. This pure sound is interrupted by mute [consonants], the true and proper arrestation of mere resonation. It is primarily through this that every sound has a meaning for itself, since the differences of mere sound in song are not determinate for themselves, but only in reference to the preceding and following sounds. Language, inasmuch as it is sonorous and articulated, is the voice of consciousness because of the fact that every sound has a meaning; that is, that in language there exists a name, the ideality of something existing, the immediate nonexistence of this.] (Hegel 5, p. 212)

Human language is the "voice of consciousness." Consciousness exists in language, and it is granted reality because language is articulated *voice*. In this articulation of the "empty" animal voice, each sound acquires a meaning, and exists as a name, as an immediate nonexistence of itself and of the thing named. But in what does this "articulation" consist? What is articulated here? Hegel responds: the "pure sound" of the animal voice, the vowel that is interrupted and arrested through the mute consonants. The articulation appears, that is, as a process of differentiation, of interruption and preservation of the animal voice. But why does this articulation of the animal voice transform it into the voice of consciousness, into memory and language? What was contained in the "pure sound" of the "empty" animal voice such that the simple articulation and preservation of this voice would give rise to human language as the voice of consciousness? Only if we examine the animal voice can we respond to this question.

In a passage from the lessons of 1805–6 Hegel returns to the problem of the animal voice:

> Stimme [ist] tätiges Gehör, reines Selbst, das sich als allgemeines setzt; Schmerz, Begierde, Freude, Zufriedenheit [ausdrückend, ist sie] Aufheben des einzelnen Selbst, dort Bewusstsein des Widerspruchs, hier Zurückgekehrtsein in sich, Gleichheit. Jedes Tier hat im gewaltsamen Tode e[ine] Stimme, spricht sich als aufgehobnes Selbst aus. (Vögel [haben] den Gesang, den die andern entbehren, weil sie dem Elemente der Luft angehören,—artikulierende Stimme, ein aufgelösteres Selbst.)
>
> In der Stimme kehrt der Sinne in sein Innres zurück; er ist negatives Selbst, Begierde. Es ist Mangel, Substanzlosigkeit an ihm selbst.

> [The voice is active hearing, purely in itself, which is posited as universal; (expressing) pain, desire, joy, satisfaction, (it is) *Aufheben* of the single itself, the consciousness of contradiction. Here it returns into itself, indifference. Every animal finds a voice in its violent death; it expresses itself as a removed-self (*als aufgehobnes Selbst*). (Birds have song, which other animals lack, because they belong to the element of air—articulating voice, a more diffused self.)
>
> In the voice, meaning turns back into itself; it is negative self, desire (*Begierde*). It is lack, absence of substance in itself.] (Hegel 4, p. 161)

Thus, in the voice, the animal expresses itself as removed: "every animal finds a voice in its violent death, it expresses itself *as aufgehobnes Selbst*."[2] If this is true, we may now understand why the articulation of the animal voice gives life to human language and becomes the voice of consciousness. The voice, as expression and memory of the animal's death, is no longer a mere, natural sign that finds its other outside of itself. And although it is not yet meaningful speech, it already contains within itself the power of the negative and of memory. Thus voice is not simply the sound of the word, which Hegel will later consider among the individual determinations of language. Rather, as a pure and originary (even if—Hegel will say—it vanishes immediately) negative articulation, the voice corresponds to the negative structure of that dimension of pure meaning that medieval logic had expressed in the notion of a "thought of the voice alone." In dying, the animal finds its voice, it exalts the soul in one voice, and, in this act, it expresses and preserves itself *as dead*. Thus, the animal voice is the *voice of death*.[3] Here the genitive should be understood in both an objective and a subjective sense. "Voice (and memory) *of death*" means: the voice is death, which preserves and recalls the living as dead, and it is, at the same time, an immediate trace and memory of death, pure negativity.

Only because the animal voice is not truly "empty" (in the passage from Hegel "empty" simply means lacking in any determinate significance), but contains the death of the animal, can human language, articulating and arresting the pure sound of this voice (the vowel)—that is to say, articulating and retaining the *voice of death*—become the *voice of consciousness*, meaningful language. A short while before, Hegel had written:

> Die Natur zu keinem dauernden Produkte [kommen] konnte, zu keiner wahrhaften Existenz. . . .nur im Tiere [gelangt sie] zum Sinne der Stimme und des Gehörs als zur unmittelbar verschwindenden Andeutung des einfach gewordenen Prozesses.
>
> [Nature could not achieve any *durable product*, it could never achieve any true existence. . . . Only in the animal does it achieve the meaning of the voice and the ear, an immediately vanishing trace of the process itself.] (Hegel 5, pp. 206-7)

Human language as articulation (that is, as arrestation and preservation) of this "vanishing trace" is the tomb of the animal voice that guards it and holds firm (*fest-halt*) its ownmost essence: "that which is most terrible (*das Furchtbarste*)," i.e., "the Dead (*das Tote*)" (Hegel 2, p. 36).

For this reason, meaningful language is truly the "life of the spirit" that "brings on" death and "is maintained" in death; and so—inasmuch as it dwells (*verweilt*) in negativity—it has the "magical power" that "converts the negative into being." But language has this power and it truly dwells in the realm of death only because it is the articulation of that "vanishing trace" that is the animal voice; that is, only because already in its very voice, the animal, in violent death, had expressed itself as removed. Because it is inscribed in voice, language is both the voice and memory of death—death that recalls and preserves death, articulation and grammar of the trace of death.

If we consider the "anthropogenetic" character that Hegel ascribes to the contact with death (Kojève 2, pp. 549-50), the importance of this situation of human language as the articulation of an animal voice that is, in truth, *the voice of death,* cannot be avoided. Why, then, does this intimate contact between language and death in human voice seem to disappear (or remain obscure) in Hegel's later writings? An indication is furnished precisely at the end of the passage cited from the 1803 lessons, where voice is explicitly placed in relation to desire (it is "negative self, desire"). In the *Phenomenology of Spirit*, as is well known, the anthropogenetic contact with death in fact takes place in the dialectic of desire and in its resolution—through the life and death battle between the master and slave—in recognition (*Anerkennen*). Here, the anthropogenetic experience of death (*die Bewahrung durch den Tod*) does not take place in a *Stimme*, in a voice, but in a *Stimmung*, the anguish and fear in the face of death. Inasmuch as it experiences fear in the face of "that absolute master" that is death, the consciousness of the slave is released from its "natural existence" (*naturliche Dasein*) and is affirmed as human consciousness, that is, as absolute negativity:

> If [consciousness] has not experienced absolute fear [*die absolute Furcht*], but only a particular fear, then the negative essence remains external to it, and its substance is not thoroughly contaminated [*durch and durch angesteckt*]. (Hegel 2, p. 155)

The slave's consciousness, now "contaminated" by the negative, develops the capacity to rein in its own desire, and by working, to form the thing, thus reaching true recognition, which, on the other hand, remains elusive for the master. The master can only satisfy his own desire in the "pure negation" of the thing, and in his enjoyment he can reach the pure feeling of himself; but his enjoyment is necessarily "only a vanishing" (*nur ein Verschwinden*), which lacks objectivity and consistency (p. 153).

A close reading of this text reveals a tight connection between the dialectics of voice and language that we reconstructed from the Jena lessons, and the dialectic of desire and work, slave and master (which the 1805–6 lessons address one directly after the other). This connection is sometimes made within Hegel's terminology: just as the voice is an "immediately vanishing trace," so the enjoyment of the master is "only a vanishing"; and as language arrests and interrupts the pure sound of the voice, so work is desire that is curbed and preserved. But the correspondence is more profound and essential and pertains both to the unique status that belongs to voice and to the master's enjoyment as figures of pure negativity and *Death*. Like the status of the voice (and of its signifying death), the status of the master (and of his enjoyment) remains obscure through the development of the Hegelian dialectic that continues, so to speak, on the part of the slave. And yet, it is precisely in the figure of the master that human consciousness emerges for the first time from natural existence and articulates its own freedom. In fact, in risking his death, the master is *recognized* by the slave. But *as what* is he recognized? Certainly not as an animal or as a natural being, because in this "trial of death" the master demonstrated the ability to renounce his natural existence; and yet, Hegel says that the slave's recognition—inasmuch as it does not derive from a being who has himself been recognized as human—is "unilateral" and insufficient to constitute the master as a true and durable human, that is, as *absolute* negativity. For this reason, his enjoyment, which even manages to complete that annihilation of the thing that desire alone could not complete, and to grant to the master "the unmitigated feeling of self," is, however, "only a vanishing." *No longer animal but not yet human, no longer desire but not yet work, the "pure negativity" of the master's enjoyment appears as the point at which the "faculty for death" (Fähigkeit des Todes) that characterizes human consciousness shows for a moment its originary articulation.* In the same way, Voice, which is no longer a natural sign and not yet meaningful discourse, is presented as the originary articulation of that "faculty for language" through which only human consciousness can grant itself lasting existence; but inasmuch as its taking place coincides with death, and Voice is the voice of death (of the "absolute master"), it is also the point, vanishing and unattainable, at which the originary articulation of the two "faculties" is completed. And as Hegel affirms in a passage from the 1805–6 lessons that will be taken up in the *Science of Logic*, "the death of the animal is the becoming of consciousness" (Hegel 4, p. 164).

Inasmuch as the Voice demonstrates this articulation of the two faculties in its initial transparency, it appears as the originary and not yet "absolved" figure of that *absolute* Idea that, as the "sole object and content of philosophy," is expressed at the end of the *Science of Logic* as the "originary word" (*das ursprüngliche Wort*). This word dwells in pure thought and it has always already "vanished" every time it is spoken:

Logic expounds the movement of the absolute Idea only as the originary *word*. This word is spoken, but in such a way that it immediately vanishes again, while it exists. The idea is, thus, only in this self-determination, in self-*perception* [*sich zu vernehmen*]; it is in *pure thought*, where difference is not yet an other-being, but it exists as transparent to itself and remains such. (Hegel 3, p. 550)[4]

Notes

1. Since Hoffmeister published the manuscripts in question, philological studies of Hegel conducted by Haering and Kimmerle have demonstrated that the lessons cannot be considered as a single draft, nor do they represent an organically planned *Realphilosophie*. Nevertheless, the 1803–4 texts with which we are concerned (in particular the section titled *III Philosophie des Geistes*) maintain a certain validity in terms of our focus. In fact, Kimmerle's analysis has shown that this section may be considered a long, unified fragment. As for the 1805–6 lessons, one can speak of a *Realphilosophie*, and the graphological analyses confirm that they were composed in the fall of 1805.

2. The connection between animal voice and negativity was already posited by Hegel in the *System der Sittlichkeit*, which Rosenzweig dates from the early summer of 1802. Hegel writes,

> "The sound of metal, the murmur of water, and the howling of the wind are not things that are transformed from inside by absolute subjectivity into their very opposites, but rather, there is a development thanks to an external movement. The animal voice derives from its punctiliousness, from its conceptual nature, and as the totality of this it belongs to the senses; if most animals scream at the danger of death, that is clearly only an expression of subjectivity."

If we recall that for Hegel, the point is a figure of negativity—in the lessons of 1805–6 it is defined as *das Dasein des Nichtdasein*, the Being-there of Non-being-there—this means that the voice arises immediately from the animal's negativity.

3. The idea of a "voice of death" as the originary language of nature was already suggested in Herder's *Abhandlung* on the origin of language (1792), which Hegel may have had in mind when he wrote the passage on voice for the lessons of 1805–6. Herder writes,

> "Who would not feel this 'Ah' penetrate through his heart, on hearing a victim of torture writhe and howl, standing before a dying being who cries out, or even before a moaning animal, when the whole living machine suffers. . . . Horror and pain cut through his bones; his whole nervous system shares the pain and destruction; the sound of death resonates [*der Todeston tönet*]. This is the chain of this language of nature!"

4. In an important passage from the *Jenenser Naturphilosophie* (Hegel 6, pp. 199-200), Ether, a figure of absolute, self-referential spirit, is described as a self-perceiving Voice:

> "Ether's ability to talk to itself is its reality; that is, it is just as infinite for itself as it is equal to itself. The equal-to-itself is the understanding [*das Vernehmen*] of infinity, just as much as it is the conception of Voice; it is the understanding, that is, the infinite, and just as absolutely reflected in itself. Ether is Spirit or the Absolute only inasmuch as it is its understanding, inasmuch as it is thus a turning in on itself. The voice that is released absolutely from inside is infinity, disruption, becoming-other-than-itself; it is perceived by the equal-to-itself that is voice-for-itself inasmuch as it is infinite. The equal-to-itself exists, it speaks; that is, it is infinite. Thus the equal-to-itself stands face to face with the speaker. Given that, infinity is Speech, and the equal-to-itself that is becoming Speech is that which understands [*das Vernehmende*]. Speech is the articulation of the sounds of the infinite that are understood by the equal-to-itself as absolute melody. These sounds are the absolute harmony of the universe, a harmony in which the equal-to-itself is mediated through the infinite with the equal-to-itself, which understands."

Excursus 4 (between the fifth and sixth days)

It is this negative articulation in its originary vanishing status that Bataille, along with the French Hegelianism of Kojève and his disciples, attempted to affirm as a possible fundamental experience beyond the horizon of the Hegelian dialectic. This affirmation of desire, of the Meinung, *the master's enjoyment, in a word, of the figures of the* Dead (das Tote)*—or, as Bataille expresses it, of "disengaged negativity"* (négativité sans emploi)*—this affirmation is perfectly legitimate, given their fundamental function, as we have seen, in the Hegelian system; but if we wish to play out this negativity against and outside of this very system, it is just as perfectly impossible.*

In fact, Hegel would have invoked the Eleusinian mystery, which he opposes to the Meinung *of sense-certainty at the beginning of the* Phenomenology, *in the face of any pretense to affirm the master's enjoyment. Certainly, sensory consciousness is the ground from which the dialectic moves, but its truth lies in being a pure nothing, unspeakable and ungraspable. And it is precisely as a nothing and a negative that the* pietas *of* Wahrnehmung *grasps this sensory consciousness in the only possible way: by uttering it in words. Similarly, the master's enjoyment seems to free itself, in its immediate vanishing, from dialectic; but it can do so only as a nothing, a vanishing, which can never be said or grasped (in this sense it is "disengaged"); the only means of speaking it or grasping it is that of the slave who guards it, as a nothing, in his work.*

Here we might say that the problem concerns the "voice" of the master. In fact, if the master truly succeeds in enjoying and in removing himself from the movement of the dialectic, he must have, in his pleasure, an animal voice (or rather, a divine voice)—precisely that which man never succeeds in finding, since he must remain trapped in meaningful discourse. (This implies that the master's enjoyment is not a human figure, but an animal, or rather a divine figure, evoking only silence, or at best, laughter.)

*The problem of "satisfaction" lies at the center of a letter from Bataille to Kojève, dated April 8, 1952 (and preserved in the Bibliothèque Nationale in Paris). Bataille begins with a warning that the terrain Kojève has chosen to explore by reproposing the idea of satisfaction is slippery (*glissant*), and leads fatally to a "farce":*

> *Il ne vous échappe pas que le terrain où vous engagez est glissant: il me semble malgré tout qu'à ne vous y engager qu'à demi, à ne pas avouer que cette satisfaction dont vous parlez n'est pas saisissable, étant en somme et du moins au sens le plus parfait une farce, vous manquez à la politesse élémentaire. . . . Il faudrait à la verité pour être complet trouver un ton indéfinissable qui ne soit ni celui de la farce ni celui du contraire et il est évident que les mots ne sortent qu'à une condition du gosier: d'être sans importance. Je crois toujours que vous minimisez l'interêt des expressions évasives que vous employez au moment où vous débouchez dans la fin de l'histoire. C'est pourquoi votre article me plaît tant, qui est la façon d'en parler la plus dérisoire—c'est-à-dire, la moins évasive.*
>
> *[It does not escape you that the terrain you are exploring is slippery: it seems to me in spite of everything that only to engage you halfway, not to avow that this satisfaction about which you speak is not graspable, since when all is said and done it is the most perfect example of a farce—this would be very impolite. . . . Truthfully, to be complete it would be necessary to find an undefinable tone, neither farcical nor its opposite, and it is obvious that the words do not come except through the functioning of the throat, voice, being of no importance. And yet I still believe that you minimize the importance of the evasive expressions you use at the moment you come to the end of history. That is why I find your article so pleasing, which is the most derisive way of speaking—that is, the least evasive.*

And at this point Bataille develops his critique of Kojève's position:

> *Seulement vous allez peut-être vite, ne vous embarassant nullement d'aboutir à une* sagesse ridicule*: il faudrait en effet représenter ce qui fait coincider la sagesse et l'objet du rire. Or je ne crois pas que vous puissiez personellement éviter ce problème dernier. Je ne vous ai jamais rien entendu dire en effet, qui ne soit expressément et volontairement comique au moment d'arriver à ce point de resolution. C'est peut-être*

la raison pour la quelle vous avez parfois accepté de faire une part à ma propre sagesse.

Malgré tout, ceci nous oppose: vous parlez de satisfaction, vous voulez bien qu'il ait de quoi rire, mais non que ce soit le principe même de la satisfaction qui soit risible.

[Perhaps you go too fast, not at all embarrassed to arrive at this laughable wisdom: in effect, one must show what makes wisdom and the object of laughter coincide. Now, I do not believe that you personally can avoid this latter problem. In effect, I never heard you say anything that was purposefully and willingly comic at the moment you arrived at this point of resolution. And perhaps that is why you have even accepted to play a role in my own wisdom.

In spite of everything, we face this problem: you speak of satisfaction, you want something to laugh about, but you ask that the very principle of satisfaction should not be laughable.]

For this reason Bataille affirms that the most correct means of posing the problem is not in terms of satisfaction, but of "sovereignty"; the sovereignty of the sage at the end of history ("en d'autres termes, en posant la souveraineté du sage à la fin de l'histoire"*), where satisfaction and dissatisfaction become identical (*"l'identité de la satisfaction et de l'insatisfaction devient sensible"*).*

In a letter to Bataille (July 28, 1942), Kojève developed a series of considerations which were in a certain sense analogous to the problem of mysticism and silence:

*Réussir à exprimer le silence (verbalement) c'est parler sans rien dire. Il y a une infinité de manières de le faire. Mais le résultat est toujours le même (si l'on réussit): le néant. C'est pourquoi toutes les mystiques authentiques se valent: dans la mésure où elles sont authentiquement mystiques, elles parlent du néant d'une façon adequate, c'est-à-dire en ne disant rien. . . . Ils (les mystiques) écrivent aussi—comme vous le faites vous-même. Pourquoi? Je pense qu'en tant que mystiques ils n'ont aucune raison de le faire. Mais je crois qu'un mystique qui écrit . . . n'est pas seulement un mystique. Il est aussi un "homme ordinaire" avec toute la dialectique de l'*Anerkennen. *C'est pourquoi il écrit. Et c'est pourquoi on trouve dans le livre mystique (en marge du silence verbalisé par le discours denué de sens) un contenu compréhensible: en particulier, philosophique. Ainsi chez vous.*

[To manage to express silence (verbally) is to speak without saying anything. There are an infinite number of ways to do it. But the result is always the same (if one is successful): nothingness. That is why all authentic mystics have value: inasmuch as they are authentically mystical, they speak of nothingness adequately, that is, they do not say

anything. . . . The mystics also write—just like you do. Why? I think that as mystics they have no reason to do it. But I believe that a mystic who writes . . . is not simply a mystic. He is also an "ordinary man" with the whole dialectic of the Anerkennen. *That is why he writes. And that is why we find in the mystical book (in the margin of silence verbalized by discourse that is stripped of meaning) a comprehensible content: in particular, a philosophical content. And so it is with you.*

Bataille characterizes what he calls "interior experience" in philosophical terms as "the contrary of action" and as the "deferral of existence until later"; but Kojève objects:

Ce qui suit est encore compréhensible et plein de sens. Mais faux. C'est-à-dire tout simplement "païen", "grec": ontologie de l'être (interminable . . .). Car vous dites: "remise de l'existence à plus tard." Mais si (comme le pensent les philosophes chrétiens) cette existence n'existe pas "plus tard"? Ou si (comme il est vrai et comme l'a dit Hegel) l'existence n'est rien d'autre que cette "remise à plus tard"? L'existence—pour parler avec Aristote (qui s'est mal compris)—est un passage de la puissance à l'acte. Quand l'acte est integral, il a épuissé la puissance. Il est sans puissance, impuissant, inexistant: il n'est plus. L'existence humaine est la remise à plus tard. Et ce "plus tard" lui-même, c'est la mort, c'est rien.

[What follows is still comprehensible and makes sense. But it is false. That is simply to say "pagan," "greek": ontology of being (interminable . . .). For you say: "deferral of existence until later." But what if (as the Christian philosophers say) this existence does not exist "later"? Or what if (as is true, and as Hegel says) existence is nothing other than this "deferral until later"? Existence—according to Aristotle (who understood incorrectly)—is the passage from potentiality to actuality. When actuality is whole, it has exhausted its potential. It is without potential, impotent, nonexistent: it is no more. Human existence is this deferral until later. And this "later" itself is death, it is nothing.]

For this reason, the closing to Kojève's letter inviting Bataille to reenter the context of Hegelian wisdom recalls the critique of Meinung *that opens the* Phenomenology*:*

Je vous souhaite donc de la puissance à l'acte, de la philosophie à la sagesse. Mais pour cela réduisez à néant ce qui n'est que néant, c'est-à-dire réduisez au silence la partie angelique de votre livre.

[I wish you thus to pass from potentiality to actuality, from philosophy to wisdom. But for that, reduce to nothingness that which is

> *only nothingness, that is, reduce to silence the angelic part of your book.]*

Any thought that wishes to think beyond Hegelianism cannot truly find a foundation, against the negative dialectic and its discourse, in the experience (mystical and, if coherent, necessarily mute) of disengaged negativity; rather, it must find an experience of speech that no longer presupposes any negative foundation. Today we live on that extreme fringe of metaphysics where it returns—as nihilism—to its own negative foundation (to its own Ab-grund, *its own ungroundedness). If casting the foundation into the abyss does not, however, reveal the* ethos, *the proper dwelling of humanity, but is limited to demonstrating the abyss of* Sigé, *then metaphysics has not been surpassed, but reigns in its most absolute form—even if this form (as Kojève suggests and as several aspects of ancient gnosis confirm, along with Bataille) is, finally, "farcical."*

The Sixth Day

Is there anything in Heidegger's thought like a ''philosophy of the Voice,'' in which the problem of the negative shows its original connection with the problem of the Voice?

We ought to say, first of all, that the problem of the voice (of the animal voice) could not be addressed in Heidegger's thought because, in construing the human as Dasein, he necessarily excludes the living being. Dasein is not a living being that has language, a *rational animal*; on the contrary, this definition is explicitly attributed to that metaphysical conception from which Heidegger attempts to keep his distance. Unlike in Hegel, the living being, the *animal*, is the thing most estranged from Being-there, ''the most difficult thing'' for Being-there to conceive:

> Of all entities, the living being [*das Lebewesen*] is probably the most difficult for us to conceive since, on the one hand, it is strictly linked with us, in a certain sense; on the other hand, however, it is also separated from our ek-sisting essence by an abyss. In comparison, it might seem that the divine essence is closer to us than the impenetrability of the living being, close in terms of an essential distance, which, as distance, is however more familiar to our ek-sisting essence than the almost inconceivable and abysmal corporeal link we share with the animal. These reflections shed a strange light on the current, rather hasty characterization of man as a *rational animal*. Since plants and animals are always already held in their environment [*Umgebung*], but never freely placed in the clearing [*Lichtung]* of

> Being—and this alone constitutes "world"—for this reason, they lack language. But they do not remain suspended without world in their environment, since language is denied to them. Rather, in this word "environment" the whole enigma of the living being is concentrated. In its essence, language is neither the manifestation of an organism nor the expression of a living being. Therefore, it never allows itself to be conceived by any means that is adequate to its essence, not on the basis of its sign-character [*Zeichencharakter*] nor, perhaps, even on the basis of its signifying character [*Bedeutungscharakter*]. Language is the clarifying-obfuscating advent of Being itself. (Heidegger 5, pp. 157-58)

Inasmuch as the living being remains held in its *Umgebung*,[1] and never appears in the *Lichtung*, it never experiences the *Da*, and this precludes the living being the word, since language is the "clarifying-obfuscating advent of Being itself." As an ek-sisting being who "bears Dasein" and "takes the *Da* into his care as the light of Being" (p. 158), man is "more than a simple man" (*mehr als der Blosse Mensch*), and, that is to say, something radically different from a *Lebewesen*, from a living being. This signifies, also, that human language has no root in a voice, in a *Stimme*: it is neither the "manifestation of an organism nor the expression of a living being," but the "advent" of Being.

If, already for Hegel, language was not simply the voice of man, but the articulation of this voice in "the voice of consciousness" through a *Voice of death*, for Heidegger there is an abyss between the living being (with his voice) and man (with his language): *language is not the voice of the living man*. Thus the essence of language cannot be determined according to the metaphysical tradition as an *articulation of (an animal) voice* and man, inasmuch as he is Dasein and not *Lebewesen*, cannot be brought to his *Da* (that is, to the place of language) by any voice. *Being Da, man is in the place of language without having a voice*. For Heidegger, every characterization of language beginning with the voice is, rather, in sympathy with metaphysics. And by conceiving language from the beginning as *phoné semantike*, metaphysics precludes any access to its true essence.

On the basis of this radical separation of language from voice, from *Stimme*, we must look to the full emergence in Heidegger's thought of the theme of the *Stimmung*. In paragraph 29 of *Sein und Zeit*, the *Stimmung* is presented as the "fundamental existential mode" in which Dasein is disclosed to itself. On the ontological level, it is the *Stimmung* that originally conveys "Being in its *Da*," and achieves the "primary discovery of the world" (*die primäre Entdeckung der Welt*, Heidegger 1, p. 138). This discovery is more originary not only than any knowledge (*Wissen*), or than any perception (*Wahrnehmen*), but it is also more originary than every state of mind in a psychological sense. (The term *Stimmung*, which we usually translate as "mood," should be stripped here of all psychological significance and restored to its etymological connection with the *Stimme*, and above all, to its originary acoustico-musical dimension; *Stimmung* appears in the German language like a translation of the Latin *concentus*, of the Greek *armonia*. From this point of view, Novalis's notion of *Stimmung*, not as a *psychology*, but as an "acoustics of the soul," is illuminating.)

Stimmung conveys Dasein before the disclosure of its *Da*. However, at the same time it reveals to Dasein its thrownness in this *Da*, its having been always already consigned to it. The originary discovery of the world is, thus, always already the unveiling of a *Geworfenheit*, a thrownness. Inherent in its structure, as we have seen, lies an essential negativity. If, in *Stimmung*, *Da* faces Dasein like an "inexorable enigma" (*unerbittliches Rätselhäftigkeit*, p. 136), that is because in revealing Dasein as always already thrown, it unveils the fact that Dasein is not brought into its *Da* of its own accord:

> As being, Dasein is something that has been thrown; it has been brought into its "there," but *not* of its own accord. As being, it has taken the definite form of a potentiality-for-Being which has heard itself and has devoted itself to itself, but *not* as itself. As existent, it never comes back behind its thrownness. . . . Although it has not *laid* that foundation *itself*, it reposes in the weight of it, which is made manifest to it as a burden by Dasein's mood (*Stimmung*). (Heidegger 1, p. 284; English ed., pp. 329-30)

If we recall that Being-the-*Da* signifies being in the place of language, that the experience of *Da* as shifter is inseparable from the instance of discourse, and that—on the other hand—for Heidegger language is not the voice of humanity, then we understand why *Stimmung*—by disclosing *Da*—reveals at the same time to Dasein, that it is never master of its ownmost Being. Dasein—since language is not its voice—can never grasp the taking place of language, it can never be its *Da* (the pure instance, the pure event of language) without discovering that it is always already thrown and consigned to discourse. In other words, *Dasein is located in the place of language without being brought there by its own voice, and language always already anticipates Dasein, because it stays without voice in the place of language*. *Stimmung* is the experience that language is not the *Stimme* of man, and so the disclosure of the world that it puts into effect is inseparable from negativity.

In paragraph 40 of *Sein und Zeit*, the determination of anxiety as the fundamental *Stimmung* carries this experience to its extreme radicality. Anxiety, which originally discloses the world and conveys Dasein before its *Da*, demonstrates, at the same time, that *Da*—which appears now like an obscure threat—is in no place, "nowhere" (*nirgends*):

> Accordingly, when something threatening brings itself close, anxiety does not "see" any definite "here" or "yonder" from which it comes. That in the face of which one has anxiety is characterized by the fact

> that what threatens is *nowhere* . . . it is already "there," and yet nowhere. In that in the face of which one has anxiety, the "It is nothing and nowhere" becomes manifest. [*Nichts ist es und nirgends*]. (p. 186; English ed., p. 231)

At the point where Dasein arrives at its ownmost disclosure, this disclosure reveals itself as a "nothing and nowhere"; *Da, the place of language is thus a nonplace* (we might think of Rilke's characterization of the Open in the eighth Duino Elegy as a *Nirgends ohne nicht*).

The negative experience of *Da*, of the taking place of language that *Stimmung* reveals, may however be more originary than that negativity that Hegel introduces through the *Diese* of sense-certainty at the beginning of the *Phenomenology*. Even the *Diese* of sensory consciousness is revealed as a *nicht-Diese* and, as we saw, the act of indication demonstrates the place of language as the having-been of voice, its vanishing and its preservation in language. But voice—in which the pretense of *Meinung* is sustained—is itself a negative that the *Wahrnehmung*, taking it as such, seizes precisely "in its truth."

On the other hand, that which *Stimmung* reveals is not simply a having-been of voice. Rather, it reveals that between language and voice there is no link, not even a negative one. Here negativity is even more radical because it does not seem to rest on a removed voice; language is not the voice of Dasein, and Dasein, thrown in *Da*, experiences the taking place of language as a nonplace (a *Nirgends*).

In paragraph 58 of *Sein und Zeit*, Heidegger addresses these premises, simultaneously posing the problem of a negativity that is more originary than the not of the dialectic (something like the *Nirgends ohne nicht* that Rilke speaks about in the context of the animal). In *What Is Metaphysics?* Heidegger explicitly confronts this theme, suggesting that the *Stimmung* of anxiety is that which places Dasein face to face with this more originary nothingness and maintains it as lost within it. The *Nichtung* one experiences here is not annihilation (*Vernichtung*) or the simple negation (*Verneinung*) of the entity, but it is an *abweisendes Verweisen*, a "repelling reference" that unveils the entity as "an absolutely other facing nothingness"; and, we might say, that is the perversion and the disappearance of all possibility of immediately indicating (*weisen*) the place of language. For this reason, in anxiety, "every saying of 'it is' remains silent" (*schweigt jedes "Ist" sagen*) and Dasein finds itself before an "empty silence" that it seeks in vain to break apart with senseless chatter (*wahlloses Reden*, Heidegger 5, pp. 9-10). If, for Heidegger, the nothingness, that is revealed in *Stimmung* is more originary than Hegelian negation, this is because it is not simply grounded in a having-been of the voice, but in a *silence* lacking any further trace of a voice. Dasein, Being-the-*Da*, signifies: to maintain oneself in the *Stimmung*, in this nothingness that is more originary than any *Stimme*, to experience a taking place of language in which all the shifters disappear, and where the *There* and the *This*, the *Da* and the *Diese*, fall to a *Nirgends*; to maintain oneself, that is, in a negativity where all possibility of indicating the taking place of language becomes obscure and collapses.

But has the program formulated in paragraph 52 of *Sein und Zeit*—an interrogation of the origin of negativity—truly been completed here? Is the nothing that the *Stimmung* of anxiety reveals in the *Da* truly more originary than that which the Hegelian critique of sense-certainty shows in the *Diese* (or than that which, in that other *Stimmung* known as "absolute fear," contaminates the slave's consciousness)? Has the Heideggerian attempt to conceive of language beyond every reference to a voice been realized, or rather, does a "philosophy of the voice," even if hidden, still rule over the Heideggerian conception of language? Has every indication, every function of the shifters, truly fallen to the *Nichtung*, or is there still some indication at work in the *abweisendes Verweisen*? And doesn't Heidegger's critique demonstrate precisely here the insufficiency of metaphysics, inasmuch as he conceives of its negativity simply in reference to a voice, while in reality metaphysics always already construes language and negativity in the most radical context of a *Voice*?

It is certain that at this point Heidegger's thought seems to reach a limit that he is unable to overcome. This limit becomes clear in the sudden reintegration of the theme of the *Stimme*, which the most originary disclosure of the *Stimmung* seemed to have completely eliminated. In paragraphs 54-62 of *Sein und Zeit*, in the disclosure of Dasein, the call (*Anruf*) of a Voice of conscience appears, and imposes a more originary comprehension (*ursprünglicher Fassen*) of this very disclosure, determined through the analysis of the *Stimmung*. The phenomenon of the call is presented as an "existential foundation" that constitutes the Being of *Da* as disclosure (p. 270). The Voice that calls is not, however, a vocal offering (*stimmliche Verlautbarung*). It does not say anything in the sense of propositional discourse, it does not say "anything about which one can speak" (p. 280), but it is a pure "giving-to-be-understood" (*zu-verstehen-geben*):

> But how are we to determine *what is said (das* Geredete) in this kind of discourse? *What* does the conscience call to him to whom it appeals? Taken strictly, nothing. . . .
>
> The call dispenses with any kind of utterance. It does not put itself into words at all; yet it does not remain obscure and indefinite. *Conscience discourses solely and constantly in the mode of keeping silent*. In this way it not only loses none of its perceptibility, but forces the Dasein which has been appealed to and summoned, into its own silence. The fact that what is called in the call has not been formulated in words, does not give this phenomenon the indefiniteness of a mysterious voice, but merely indicates that our understanding of what is

"called" is not to be tied up with an expectation of anything like a communication. (pp. 273-74; English ed., p. 318)

Like the *vox sola* of medieval logic, the giving-to-be-understood of the Voice is a pure intention to signify without any concrete advent of signification; a pure meaning that says nothing. And, just as a *cogitatio,* as pure will to understand (*conatus*) without any determinate understanding, corresponded to the *vox sola* of Gaunilo, so in *Sein und Zeit*, a *Gewissen-haben-Wollen*, a desire-to-have-conscience that is anterior to any particular "conscience of" corresponds to the *zu-verstehen-geben*.

For Heidegger, that which calls in the experience of the Voice is Dasein itself, from the depths of its loss in *Stimmung*. Having reached the limit, in its anxiety, of the experience of its being thrown, without a voice in the place of language, Dasein finds *another Voice*, even if this is a Voice that calls only in the mode of silence. Here, the paradox is that the very absence of voice in Dasein, the very "empty silence" that *Stimmung* revealed, now reverses itself into a Voice and shows itself as always already determined and attuned (*gestimmt*) by a Voice. More originary than the thrownness without voice in language is the possibility to understand the call of the Voice of conscience; more originary than the experience of *Stimmung* is that of *Stimme*. And it is only in relation to the call of the Voice that this ownmost disclosedness of Dasein, which paragraph 60 presents as a "self-thrownness into the ownmost culpability, tacit and capable of anxiety," is revealed. If guilt stemmed from the fact that Dasein was not brought into its *Da* of its own accord and was, thus, the foundation of negativity, then, through the comprehension of the Voice, *Dasein*, now decided, assumes the function of acting as the "negative foundation of its own negativity." It is this double negativity that characterizes the structure of the Voice and constitutes it as the most original and *negative* (that is, abysmal) metaphysical foundation. Without the call of the Voice, even the authentic decision (which is essentially a "letting-oneself-be-called," *sich vorrufenlassen*) would be impossible, just as it would be impossible for Dasein to assume its ownmost and insuperable possibility: death.

Here the theme of the Voice demonstrates its inextricable connection to that of death. Only inasmuch as Dasein finds a Voice and lets itself be called by this Voice, can it accede to that Insuperable that is the possibility to not be *Da*, to not be the place of language. If Dasein is simply thrown without voice into the place of language, then it will never be able to rise above its having been thrown in *Da* and thus, it will never be able to authentically think death (which is precisely the possibility of not being the *Da*); but if on the other hand it finds a Voice, then it can rise up to its insuperable possibility and *think death*: it can *die* (*sterben*) and not simply *cease* (*ableben*). For this reason, "the authentic thinking of death" is defined, in paragraph 62, as an "existential wanting-to-have-a-conscience, which has become transparent to itself, that is, with the very terms that define the comprehension of the Voice. *Thinking death is simply thinking the Voice.* Turning radically back, in death, from its having been thrown into *Da*, Dasein negatively retrieves its own aphonia. The silent call of a Voice is thus maintained even in the most extreme and abysmal possibility, the possibility of not being the *Da*, the possibility that language does not take place. Just as, for Hegel, the animal finds its voice in violent death, so Dasein, in its authentic Being toward death, finds a Voice: and as in Hegel, this Voice preserves the "magic power" that inverts the negative into being; it demonstrates, that is, that nothingness is only the "veil" of being.

In *What Is Metaphysics?* and especially in the *Afterword* added to the fourth edition in 1943, the recuperation of the theme of the Voice is completed. The *Stimmung* of anxiety appears here as comprehensible only in reference to a *lautlose Stimme*, a voice without sound that "attunes us (*stimmt*) to the terror of the abyss." Anxiety is nothing more than *die von jene Stimme gestimmt Stimmung*, the vocation (as we might translate it in order to maintain the etymological development) attuned to that Voice (Heidegger 5, p. 102). And the "Voice without sound" is the Voice of Being (*Stimme des Seins*) that calls man to experience Being, in nothingness:

> Einzig der Mensch unter allem seienden er fährt, angerufen von der Stimme des Seins, das Wunder aller Wunder: dass Seiendes ist. Der also in seinem Wesen in die Wahrheit des seins gerufene ist daher stets in einer Wesentlichen Weise gestimmt. Der klare Mut zur wesenhaften Angst verbürgt die geheimnisvolle Möglichkeit der Erfahrung des Seins.
>
> [Man alone of all beings, when addressed by the Voice of Being, experiences the marvel of all marvels: that the entity *is*. Therefore the being that is called in its very essence to the truth of Being is always attuned in an essential sense. The clear courage for essential anxiety guarantees that most mysterious of all possibilities: the experience of Being.] (Heidegger 5, p. 103; English ed., p. 386)

So the experience of Being is the experience of a Voice that calls without saying anything, and human thought and words are born merely as an "echo" of this Voice:

> Das anfängliche Denken ist der Widerfall der Gunst des Seins, in der sich das Einzige lichtet und sich ereignen lässt: dass Seindes ist. Dieser Widerhall ist die menschliche Antwort auf das Wort der lautlosen Stimme, des Seins. Die Antwort des Denkens ist der Ursprung des menschlichen Wortes, welches Wort erst die Sprache als die Verlautung des Wortes in die Wörter entstehen lässt.
>
> [Original thinking is the echo of Being's favor wherein it clears a

space for itself and causes the unique occurrence: that the entity is. This echo is man's answer to the Word of the soundless Voice of Being. The speechless answer of his thinking through sacrifice is the origin of the human word, which is the prime cause of language as the enunciation of the Word in words.] (Heidegger 5, p. 105; English ed., p. 389)

The Heideggerian program for conceiving of language beyond every *phone* has thus not been maintained. And if metaphysics is not simply that thought that thinks the experience of language on the basis of an (animal) voice, but rather, if it always already thinks this experience on the basis of the negative dimension of a Voice, then Heidegger's attempt to think a "voice without sound" beyond the horizon of metaphysics falls back inside this horizon. Negativity, which takes place in this Voice, is not a more originary negativity, but it does indicate this, according to the status of the supreme shifter that belongs to it within metaphysics, the taking place of language and the disclosure of the dimension of Being. The experience of the Voice—conceived as pure and silent meaning and as pure wanting-to-have-a-conscience—once again reveals its *fundamental* ontological duty. Being is the dimension of meaning of Voice as the taking place of language, that is, of pure meaning without speech and of pure wanting-to-have-a-conscience without a conscience. The thought of Being is the thought of the Voice.

Thus, in the essay on *The Origin of the Work of Art*, Heidegger evokes the resoluteness intended in *Sein und Zeit* and presents it (as, in essence, a "letting-oneself-be-called by the Voice") on the horizon of will; not as a will to anything or as the decisive action of a subject, but as the "opening up of Dasein, out of its captivity in the entity, to the openness of Being," that is, as the experience of the Voice in its capacity as supreme shifter and originary structure of transcendence (Heidegger 2, p. 55; English ed., p. 67). And in *The Question of Being*, the dimension of Being is defined as *Zusammengehören von Ruf und Gehör*, "belonging-together of the call and hearing," that is, again, as experience of the Voice (Heidegger 5, p. 236).

It should not surprise us that, as in every conception of the event of language that places in a Voice its originary taking place and its negative foundation, language remains even here metaphysically divided into two distinct planes: first *die Sage*, the originary and silent speech of Being, which, inasmuch as it coincides with the very taking place of language and with the disclosure of the world, shows itself (*zeight sich*), but remains unspeakable for human words; and second, human discourse, the "word of mortals," which can only respond to the silent Voice of Being. The relation between these two planes (the taking place of language and that which is said within it, Being and entity, world and thing) is once again governed by negativity; the demonstration of *Sage* is unnameable in terms of human language. (There is no word, the essay on George will say, for the word itself. Discourse cannot speak its taking place; Heidegger 3, p. 192.) This can only correspond (*ent-sprechen*, ''un-speak'') with *Sage* through its own disappearance, venturing, like the word of the poets, to that limit where the silent experience of the taking place of language in the Voice and in death is completed (*sie*—the poets—*wagen die Sprache*, Heidegger 2, p. 286). The double nature of showing and signifying in the Western conception of language thus confirms its originary ontological significance.

Note

1. Why does Heidegger write, ''in this word *Umgebung* the whole enigma of the living being is concentrated''? In the word *Umgebung* (the circumscription, the inscription all around) we should hear the verb *geben*, which is, for Heidegger, the only appropriate verb for Being: *es gibt Sein,* Being is given. That which ''is given'' around the animal is Being. The animal is circumscribed by Being; but, precisely for this reason, he is always already held in this *giving*. He does not interrupt it, he can never experience the *Da,* that is, the taking place of Being and language. On the other hand, man *is* the *Da,* and in language he experiences the advent (*Ankunft*) of Being. This Heideggerian passage engages in an intimate dialogue with the eighth Duino Elegy of Rilke, and the two should be read together. Here man, who sees only ''World,'' is contrasted with the animal ''who looks into the Open with all of his eyes''; and while for the animal Being is ''infinite'' and ''misunderstood,'' and dwells in a ''No-place without a not'' (*Nirgends ohne nicht*), man can only ''be face to face'' in a ''Destiny.''

Excursus 5 (between the sixth and seventh days)

The mythogeme of a silent voice as the ontological foundation of language already appears in late-antique Gnostic and Christian mysticism. In the Corpus Hermeticum *I.31, God is invoked as "unspeakable and inexpressible" (*aneklalete, arrhete*), and yet he is "spoken with the voice of silence" (*siope phonoumene*). In this context, the Gnostic figure of* Sigé *is particularly significant for its fundamental function in Valentinian gnosis and for its seminal role in Christian mysticism and philosophy.*

*In Valentinian gnosis, the Abyss (*buthos*)—incomprehensible, unformed, and eternally pre-existent—contains within itself a thought (*Ennoia*) that is silent,* Sigé. *And this "silence" is the primary, negative foundation of revelation and of* logos, *the "mother" of all that is formed from the Abyss. In a dense fragment from the* Excerpta ex Theodato *the Valentinians write:*

> *Silence (*Sigé*), as the mother of all things that have been emitted from the Abyss, says nothing about the unspeakable. That which it has understood, it has called incomprehensible. [*o men ouk eschen eipein peri tou arreton sesigeken, o de katelaben, touto akatalepton prosegorensen.*]*

Thus, Silence comprehends the Abyss as incomprehensible. Without Sigé *and its silent thought, the Abyss could not even have been considered incomprehensible or unspeakable. Inasmuch as Silence negatively unveils the arch-original dimension of the Abyss to sense and to signification, it is the mystical foundation of every possible revelation and every language, the original language of God as*

Abyss (in Christian terms, the figure of the dwelling of logos *in* arche, *the original place of language). In a codex by Nag-Hammadi (VI 14.10), silence is in fact explicitly placed in relation to voice and language in their original dimension:*

I am unreachable
silence
and the Epinoia
about which much is remembered.
I am the voice
which gives many sounds their origin
and the Logos
which has many images.
I am the pronunciation of my name.

*It is with an apocryphal Christian (*Mart. Petri *X) that the status of silence as Voice, through which the spirit is joined to Christ, finally finds its most clear expression:*

*I thank you . . . not with the tongue which utters truth and falsity, nor with that speech which is spoken by the technique of material nature, but I thank you, O King, with the voice which is known through silence (*dia siges nooumene*), which is not heard in the visible world, which is not produced with the organs of the mouth, which does not enter carnal ears, which is not heard in perishable substance, which is not in the world and is not placed on earth nor written in books, which does not belong to one, nor does it not belong to one; I thank you, Jesus Christ, with the silence of that same voice by which the spirit in me urges me to love you, to speak to you, to see you.*

A shadow of the figure of Sigé, *of the silence of God as abysmal foundation of the word, is also present in later Christian theology and mysticism in the idea of the silent Word, which dwells as unspeakable in the intellect of the Father (*Verbum quod est in silentio paterni intellectus, Verbum sine verbo, *Meister Eckhart will write). Already Saint Augustine posited a correspondence between this dwelling, this "birth" of the Word in the Father, and the experience of a silent word, "which does not belong to any language":*

Verbum autem nostrum, illud quod non habet sonum nec cogitationem soni, sed eius rei quam videndo intus dicimus, et ideo nullius linguae est; atque inde utcumque simile est in hoc enigmate illi Verbo Dei; quod etiam Deus est, quoniam sic et hoc de nostra nascitur, quemadmodum et illud de scientia patris natum est.

[But that word of ours which has neither sound nor thought of

> *sound, is the word of that thing which we inwardly speak by seeing it, and therefore, it belongs to no language; hence in this enigma there is a likeness, be it what it may, to that Word of God who is also God, since it is also born from our knowledge as that Word was born from the knowledge of the Father.] (Augustine, De Trinitate 15, 14.24; English ed., p. 487)*

In its silent "spiritual prayer," the Syrian mystical tradition will seize upon this experience, recounting how a praying man arrives at a place where the language is "more internal than words" and "more profound than lips," a language of "silence" and "stupor." Thus there is no absolute opposition between the Gnostic Sigé *and Christian* logos, *which are never completely separated. Silence is simply the negative foundation of* logos, *its taking place and its unknown dwelling (according to Johannine theology), in the* arche *that is the Father. This dwelling of* logos *in* arche *(like that of* Sigé *in* Buthos*) is an abysmal dwelling—that is, ungrounded—and Trinitarian theology never manages to fully emerge from this abysmalness.*

The Seventh Day

The attempt at taking-the-*This*, at grasping negatively the very taking place of language in the unspeakable experience of the Voice, constitutes—as we saw—the fundamental experience of that which, in Western culture, we term "philosophy." Now we must ask if there is another experience of language within this culture that does not rest on an unspeakable foundation. If philosophy is presented from the beginning as a "confrontation" with (*enantiosis*) and a divergence from (*diaphora*, Plato, *Republic* 607b-c) poetry (we should not forget that Plato was a tragic poet who decided to burn his tragedies at a certain point, and, seeking a new experience of language, composed those Socratic dialogues that Aristotle mentions along with the Mimes of Sophrones as a true and proper literary genre), then what is the extreme experience of language within the poetic tradition? Do we find in the poetic tradition, unlike the philosophical tradition, a language that does not rest on the negative foundation of its own place? And where do we encounter something like a reflection on the taking place of language in the Western poetic tradition?

Within this context we will now read two poetic texts, both of which treat this very experience of the advent of the poetic word. The first is a Provençal text from the beginning of the thirteenth century, the *tenso de non-re*, the "tenson of nothing," by Aimeric de Peguilhan, a troubadour whom Dante names and admires in the *De vulgari eloquentia*, citing his work as an example of the highest poetic construction.

In ancient rhetoric, the term *topics* referred to a technique of the originary advents of language; that is, a technique of the "places" (*topoi*) from which human discourse arises and begins. According to this tradition of thought, which enjoyed a dominant position in humanist culture up until the threshold of the modern age, the dimension of *ratio* (or *ars*) *iudicandi*, that is to say the science—logic—that assures the truth and correctness of propositions, is less originary than that of the *ratio* (or *ars*) *inveniendi*, which sets off the very advent of discourse and assures the possibility of "finding" language, of reaching its place. Whereas the doctrine of judgment does not have originary access to the place of language, but can only be constituted on the basis of an already-having-been-given of language, *topics* conceived of its duty as the construction of a place for language, and this place constituted the *argument*. The term *argumentum* derives from the very theme *argu*, found in *argentum* and signifying "splendor, clarity." *To argue* signified originally, "to make shine, to clarify, to open a passage for light." In this sense, the argument is the illuminating event of language, its taking place.

And yet the ancient *topics*—inasmuch as it was especially concerned with the orator and his constant need for arguments at his disposition—was not (nor could it be) up to this task, and it eventually eroded into a mnemonic device, conceiving of the "places" as mnemonic images. This technique assured the orator of the possibility to "argue" his discourse. As a technique of memory places (*loci*), *topics* no longer experienced the events of language, but was limited to constructing an artificial dwelling (a "memorial") in which these events were fixed as always already given and completed. In fact, ancient rhetoric (like logic itself)[1] conceives of language as always already given, as something that has always already taken place; for the speaker it is simply a matter of fixing and memorizing this being-already-given in order to make it available. This is precisely the duty of the *ratio inveniendi*.

Around the twelfth century, the ancient *topics* and its *ratio inveniendi* were reinterpreted in a radically new way by the Provençal poets, giving rise to modern European poetry. For the Provençal poets, the *ratio inveniendi* was transformed into *razo de trobar*, and they took their name from this expression (*trobador* and *trobairitz*); but in the passage from the Latin *invenire* to the Provençal *trobar*, there was much more at stake than a simple terminological mutation. According to the etymologists, the Provençal *trobar* derives, through the popular Latin *tropare* and the late Latin *attropare*, from the Latin *tropus*, meaning rhetorical figure; or more probably, from *tropus* in its musical connotation, indicating a song inserted in the liturgy. The etymological investigation, however (even if it suggests that *trobar*, "to find," indicates the experience of language appropriate to music and poetry), is, by itself, insufficient to confirm the mutation at stake here.

As we have seen, the *inventio* of classical rhetoric presupposed the event of language as always already completed; it was only a matter of reinventing, in this being-given, the "arguments" it contained. The first seeds of change in this conception of the *inventio*, sowed during that radical transformation of the experience of language that was Christianity, are already evident in Augustine's *De Trinitate*, where *inventio* is interpreted as *"in id venire quod quaeritur"* (*"unde et ipsa quae appellatur inventio, si verbi originem retractemus, quid aliud resonat, nisi quia invenire est in id venire quod quaeritur?"* X 7.10). Here man is not always already in the place of language, but he must come into it; he can only do this through *appetitus,* some amorous desire, from which the word can be born if it is united with knowledge. The experience of the event of language is, thus, above all an amorous experience. And the word itself is *cum amore notitia*, a union of knowledge and love: *"cum itaque se mens novit et amat, iungitur ei amore verbum eius. Et quoniam amat notitiam et novit amorem, et verbum in amore et amor in verbo, et utrumque in amante et dicente"* (IX 10.15). The "birth of the mind," from which the word is born, is thus preceded by desire, which remains in a state of agitation until the object of desire is found (*"porro appetitus ille, qui est in quaerente, procedit a quaerente, et pendet quodammodo, neque requiescat fine quo inteditur, nisi id quod quaeritur inventum quaerenti copuletur*" IX 12.18). According to this conception, the amorous desire from which the word is born is more originary than *inventio* as a rememorization of the being-given of the word.

With the Provençal poets, the classical *topics* is already definitively surpassed. What they experience as *trobar* goes definitively beyond *inventio*. The troubadours do not wish to recall arguments already in use by a *topos*, but rather they wish to experience the *topos* of all *topoi*, that is, the very taking place of language as originary *argument*, from which only arguments in the sense of classical rhetoric may derive. Thus, the *topos* can no longer be a place of memory in the mnemonic sense. Now it is presented in the traces of the Augustinian *appetitus* as a place of love. *Amors* is the name the troubadours gave to the experience of the advent of the poetic word and thus, for them, love is the *razo de trobar* par excellence.

It is difficult to understand the sense in which the poets understood love, as long as we obstinately construe it according to a secular misunderstanding, in a purely biographical context. For the troubadours, it is not a question of psychological or biographical events that are successively expressed in words, but rather, of the attempt to *live the topos itself, the event of language as a fundamental amorous and poetic experience*. In the verses of one of the oldest troubadours, Jaufré Rudel, this transformation of the *razo* is programmatically uttered as an "understanding of the *razo* in itself":

No sap chantar qui so non di,
ni vers trobar qui motz no fa,
ni conois de rima cos va
si razo non enten en si.

Only later, when this original linking of love and *razo* in the poetic experience ceased to be comprehensible, did love become a sentiment, one *Stimmung* among others that the poet could put into poetry if he so desired. The modern idea of a *lived reality* as the material that the poet must express in his poetry (an unfamiliar notion in the classical world, which, instead, made use of topics and rhetoric) is born precisely from this misunderstanding of the troubadour (and later *stilnovo*) experience of the *razo*. (The equivocation that persists in assigning a biographical experience to the dimension of the *razo* is so old that it already forms the basis of the first attempts at explaining Provençal lyrics—those *razos* and *vidas* composed between the thirteenth and fourteenth centuries in Provençal, but within an Italian environment. In these early novelettes, the earliest examples of biography in a Romance language, a true and proper reversal of the poetry-life relationship that characterizes the poetic experience of the *razo* takes place. That which for the troubadours was a *living* of the *razo*—that is, an experiencing of the event of language as love—now becomes a *reasoning the life,* a putting into words of biographical events. But a careful analysis reveals that in reality the authors of the *razos* do nothing more than carry the troubadours' process to its extreme consequences; in fact, they construct a biographical anecdote to explain a poem, but here the *lived* is invented or "found" on the basis of the *poetic* and not vice versa, as will be the case when the troubadour project has long been forgotten. How does this attempt, which not by chance takes place in an Italian environment, come to characterize in an exemplary fashion the typically Italian concept of life as *fable*, making biography in a strict sense impossible? This is a question that cannot be answered in the present study.)

Yet this experience of the taking place of language as love necessarily included a negativity that the most radical troubadours—following contemporary theological speculations on the concept of *nihil*—did not hesitate to conceive of in terms of nothingness.

Farai un vers de dreyt nien

begins a poem by William IX, Duke of Aquitaine, generally thought to be the first and most illustrious of the troubadours. The place from which and in which the poetic word comes into being is presented here as something that can only be indicated negatively. To sing, "to find," becomes, thus, to experience the *razo*, the event of language as *irretrievable*, pure nothingness (*dreyt nien*). And if love is presented in the Provençal lyric as a desperate adventure whose object is far away, unattainable, and yet accessible only in this distance, that is because the experience of the taking place of language is at stake here, and this experience, as such, seems necessarily to be marked by negativity.

But now let us read the *tenso* of Aimeric de Peguilhan:

Amics Albertz, tenzos soven
fan assatz tuit li trobador,
e partisson razon d'amor
e d'als, qan lur platz, eissamen.
Mas ieu faz zo q'anc om non fes,
tenzon d'aizo qi res non es;
q'a razon pro'm respondrias,
mas al nien vueil respondatz;
et er la tenzos de non-re.

N'Aimerics, pueis del dreg nien
mi voletz far respondedor,
non voil autre razonador
mas mi meteus. Mon eiscien,
be'm par q'a razon respondes
qi respon zo qe res non es.
Us nienz es d'autre compratz.
Per q'al nien don m'apellatz,
respondrai com? Calarai me!

Albertz, ges callan non enten
qe'l respondres aja valor;
ni mutz non respon a segnor,
e mutz non diz vertat ni men.
S'ades callatz, con respondres?
Ja parlei, qe'us ai escomes.
Nient a nom; donc, si'l nomatz,
parlares, mal grat qe n'ajatz,
o no'i respondretz mal ni be.

N'Aimerics, nuil essernimen
no'us aug dir, anz parlatz error.
Folia deu hom a follor
respondre, e saber a sen.
Eu respon a non sai qe s'es
con cel q'en cisterna s'es mes,
qe mira sos oils e sa faz,
e s'el sona, sera sonatz
de si meteus, c'als non i ve.

Albertz, cel sui eu veramen
qi son'e mira sa color,
et aug la voz del sonador,

pueis ieu vos son primeiramen;
e'l resonz es nienz, so'm pes:
donc es vos—e no'us enoi ges—
nienz, s'aissi respondiatz.
E si per tal vos razonatz,
ben es fols qi de ren vos cre.

N'Aimerics, d'entrecimamen
sabetz, e fai vos hom lauzor;
si no'us entendon li pluzor,
ni vos mezeus, zo es parven.
Et es vos en tal razon mes
don ieu issirai, mal qe'us pes,
e vos remanretz essaratz;
e sitot mi matracrjatz,
ieu vos respon, mas no'us dic qe.

Albertz, zo q'eu vos dic vers es:
donc dic eu qe om ve non-res,
qar s'un flum d'un pont fort gardatz,
l'ueil vos diran q'ades anatz,
e l'aiga can cor s'i rete.

N'Aimerics, non es mals ni bes,
aizo de qe'us es entremes,
q'atrestam petit issegatz
co'l molinz q'a roda de latz,
qe's mou tot jorn e non vai re.

[Friend Albert, all the troubadours compose *tenzos* often and propose a *razo* of love or of something else, likewise, when it pleases them. But I am composing what no one ever made,—a *tenso* about nothing. You would answer well to a *razo*; but I wish you to answer to nothing. So this *tenso* will be about nothing.

Sir Aimeric, since you wish to make me an answerer to a mere nothing, I do not wish to have any other debater but myself. In my opinion, I think that he makes a good reply who answers that it is nothing. One nothing balances the other. Since then you invite me to a debate about nothing, how shall I answer? I'll keep silent.

Sir Albert, I don't think that a silent answer is worth anything. A dumb man does not answer his lord, nor speak the truth nor lie. If you keep silent all the time, how will you answer? I have spoken to you already, for I challenged you. Nothingness has a name; therefore, if you name it, you'll speak in spite of yourself, or you will not answer the challenge either well or ill.

Sir Aimeric, I don't hear you speak with discernment; on the contrary, you talk erroneously. One should answer foolishness with folly, wisdom with sense. So I answer this "I don't know what" like a man in a cistern who looks at his own eyes and face; and if he utters a word, he will be echoed by himself, for he doesn't see anything else in it.

Sir Albert, that is who I am really, a man who speaks and looks at his own face; and I hear the voice of the speaker, for I speak to you first. But the echo is nothing, as I think. So you are—and don't let this irk you—nothing, if you answer thus. And if you argue yourself into that quandary, he is a fool who believes you about anything.

Sir Aimeric, you do know confusing arguments, and people praise you for that, even if most of them do not understand you—nor do you understand yourself, it seems. And you have got yourself into a *razo* that I will get out of, however it irk you; and you will remain stuck in it. Though you knock me down, I answer—but I do not say a word.

Sir Albert, what I tell you is true. I tell you that one can see nothing; for if you watch a river closely from a bridge, your eyes will tell you that it is you who are moving and that a running water is still.

Sir Aimeric, this thing that you challenged me to debate is neither good nor bad. You won't get anywhere with it, any more than a mill with a wheel beside it, which turns night and day and doesn't go anywhere.] (English ed., *The Poems of Aimeric de Peguilhan*, trans. William Shephard and Frank Chambers. Evanston, Ill.: Northwestern University Press, 1950)

The poem is presented as a reflection on the *razo*, on the advent of the poetic word. As earlier, in the *vers* of William IX, the *razo* is no longer simply a *razo d'amor*, an experience of love and its dictation as the originary place of the word; instead, the *razo* is now *aizo qi res non es*, that is, nothing. The tenson invites a reader to experience the place of language as nothing as it speaks from this nothing, so it is a *tenzo de non-re*, a tenson of no-thing. The poets who compete in this tenson experience the event of language as if they were called to speak from nothing and to respond to nothing (*del dreg nien/mi voletz far respondedor*). In the second stanza, Albert (the troubadour Albert de Sestaro) seems to identify the response to the *razo* of nothing in silence. To respond to nothing—he says—signifies understanding that no one has called him to speak, that there is no other *razonador* but *mi meteus* and, consequently, to be silent (*calarai me*). Thus a nothing is "balanced" by another nothing.

However, in the following stanza, Aimeric excludes the possibility that silence is an experience suited to nothingness as *razo*. Nothingness, he says, has a name;

and so, by the simple act of speaking the name, one enters into language and speaks about nothing. Human language speaks about nothing and on the basis of nothing because it names nothing and thus, it has always already responded to it. Here Aimeric takes up the discussions of the nature of nothing that, in medieval thought, found their first exemplary expression during the ninth century in the *Epistula de nihilo et de tenebris* by Fridegodus of York. In asking whether nothing is something or not (*nihilne aliquid sit an non*), Fridegodus concluded that nothing is something, because whatever response one might give to the question, nothing, since it is spoken as a noun, must necessarily refer to an *aliquid* that it signifies. This *aliquid* is a *magnum quiddam* according to the Abbott of York, by virtue of the fact that "the divine power created the earth, water, fire, and light, the angels and the human soul from nothing." During the course of the Middle Ages, these speculations even received a popular form, for example, in the collection of riddles titled *Disputatio Pippini cum Albino*. Here the being of nothingness is investigated even more subtly than in the epistle of Fridegodus, and its status of existence is made precise through the opposition of *nomen* and *res*:

> ALBINUS. Quod est quod est et non est?
> PIPPINUS. Nihil.
> A. Quomodo potest esse et non esse?
> P. Nomine est et re non est.
> [ALBINUS. What is and yet is not?
> PIPPINUS. Nothing.
> A. How can it be and not be?
> P. It is in name and it is not in substance.]

We have already encountered something similar to this form of being in *nomine* and not in *re* in the theological reflections of Gaunilo. The dimension of meaning of nothing is, in fact, quite close to the dimension of meaning that Gaunilo expressed as the *esse in voce* and as the thought of the voice alone (*cogitatio secundum vocem solam*). Similarly, nothing is a sort of limiting dimension within language and signification. It is the point at which language ceases to signify the *res*, without, however, becoming a simple thing among others, because, as a pure name and pure voice, it now simply indicates itself. Inasmuch as it opens a dimension where language exists but signified things do not, the field of meaning of nothing appears close to that of the shifters that indicate the very taking place of language, the instance of discourse, independently of what is said. With respect to shifters, the field of meaning of nothing is presented as a sort of supreme shifter. As being, it takes up the very negative structure of the Voice, which we saw was inherent in the functioning of the shifters. (In fact, the linguistic expression of nothing is almost always presented as the negation of a shifter or of one of the *transcendentia* from medieval logic: in Italian, *niente*; French, *néant* = *nec-entem*; Old French, *ne-je*, *nennil* = *ne-je*, *ne-n-il*; German, *nichts* = *ni-wiht*; English, nothing = no-thing; Latin, *nullus* = *ne-ullus*.)

In the fourth stanza of the *tenso*, the experience of speaking from nothing about nothing is presented, in fact, as the experience of the field of meaning of the shifter "I"; an experience, that is, of reflection in which the speaking subject—captured, according to a model that was common in medieval poetry, in the figure of Narcissus—sees himself and hears his own voice. (To respond to nothing is to act "like a man in a cistern who looks at his own eyes and face and if he utters a word, he will be echoed by himself.") In Aimeric's response this experience of the I is pushed to the most extreme consciousness of the exclusive, negative position of the I in the instance of discourse. I is always only he who speaks and sees his own face reflected in the water, but neither the reflection nor the echo of the voice—which are simply nothing—can sustain him or guarantee him consistency beyond the single instance of discourse (this is precisely the tragedy of Narcissus). And in the final stanzas, the experience of the poetic *razo* as nothing is translated (as in the *envoi* of a famous canzone by Arnaut Daniel) into a series of contradictory images where the speech act is represented as an incessant movement that goes nowhere and is in no place.

We have dwelt so long on this Provençal *tenso* because the experience of the *razo*, of the originary advent of poetic language that is at stake here, seems singularly close to the negative experience of the place of language that we encountered as fundamental in the Western philosophical tradition. Even poetry seems here to experience the originary event of its own word as *nothing*. The poetic and philosophical experiences of language are thus not separated by an abyss, as an ancient tradition of thought would have it, but both rest originally in a common negative experience of the taking place of language. Perhaps, rather, only from this common negative experience is it possible to understand the meaning of that scission in the status of language that we are accustomed to call poetry and philosophy; and thus, to understand that which, while separating them, also holds them together and seems to point beyond their fracture.

In this context we will now read a second text, the idyll titled *L'infinito* by Giacomo Leopardi:

Sempre caro mi fu quest'ermo colle,
e questa siepe, che da tanta parte
dell'ultimo orizzonte il guardo esclude.
Ma sedendo e mirando, interminati
spazi di là da quella, e sovrumani
silenzi, e profondissima quiete
io nel pensier mi fingo; ove per poco
il cor non si spaura. E come il vento

odo stormir tra queste piante, io quello
infinito silenzio a questa voce
vo comparando: e mi sovvien l'eterno,
e le morte stagioni, e la presente
e viva, e il suon di lei. Cosi tra questa
immensità s'annega il pensier mio:
e il naufragar m'è dolce in questo mare.

[This lonely knoll was ever dear to me,
and this hedgerow that hides from view
so large a part of the remote horizon.
But as I sit and gaze my thought conceives
interminable spaces lying beyond that
and supernatural silences
and profoundest calm, until my heart
almost becomes dismayed. And I hear
the wind come rustling through these leaves,
I find myself comparing to this voice
that infinite silence: and I recall eternity
and all the ages that are dead
and the living presence and its sounds. And so
in this immensity my thought is drowned:
and in this sea is foundering sweet to me.]
(English ed., pp. 147-48)

The demonstrative pronoun *this* is repeated six times in the poem always at a decisive moment (and two times we find *that*, which is strictly correlated). It is as if continually, in the space of its fifteen lines, the poem manages to perform the gesture of indication, throwing itself onto a *this* that it tries to demonstrate and grasp: from "this knoll," with which the idyll opens, to "these leaves" and "this voice," which cause a turn in the discourse, up to "this immensity" and "this sea" where it concludes. And always from the experience of the *this* derives the dismayed sense of the interminable, of the infinite, as if the gesture of indication, of saying "this," caused the incommensurable, silence, or fear to arise in the idyll; and at the end, reflection is placated and sinks into a final "this." In addition, the grammatical correlative regulating the alternation between *this* and *that* seems to assume a particular significance in the course of the poem. The *this* of the second line, indicating that which is dear and familiar and protects the gaze from what may lie beyond, is reversed in line 5 into a *that*, beyond which the interminable and fearful space *of there* is unveiled. And, in line 13 it is *that*—the infinite silence of line 10—which again yields to a *this* (the immensity in which reflection is annihilated).

What does *this* signify here? And can we truly understand the idyll *L'infinito* without experiencing the *this* as it constantly invites us to do? If we keep in mind what we have said in the last few days concerning the field of meaning of *this* and the ways in which, as an indicator of utterance, *this* cannot be understood outside of a reference to the instance of discourse, then we can see in the idyll a discourse in which the sphere of the utterance, with its formal apparatus of shifters, appears dominant. We might say that in a certain way the idyll carries out a central experience, the experience of the instance of discourse, as if it incessantly attempts to grasp the very taking place of language. But what do we learn of the shifter *this* in our reading of the idyll, which we had not already learned through linguistics and the philosophical tradition? In other words, how is the problem of the utterance and the taking place of language posed in a poetic text?

First, the poem seems to always already assume a certain characteristic of the *This*—both universal and negative—which had guided the Hegelian critique of sense-certainty. If, for a moment, "this" knoll and "this" hedgerow seem, in fact, to be comprehensible only in an indissoluble existential relation with the moment at which Leopardi pronounces (or writes) the idyll for the first time, having before his eyes a determinate knoll or hedgerow, a few seconds of reflection suffice to convince us of the opposite. Certainly the poem *L'infinito* was written to be read and repeated innumerable times and we understand it perfectly without retreating to that place on the outskirts of Recanati (supposing that such a place has ever existed), represented in some photographs accompanying various editions of the text: the knoll of *L'infinito*. Here the particular status of the utterance in poetic discourse shows the character that constitutes the foundation of its ambiguity and its transmissibility. The instance of discourse to which the shifter refers is the very taking place of language in general—that is, in our case, the instance of discourse in which any speaker (or reader) repeats (or reads) the idyll *L'infinito*. As in the Hegelian analysis of sense-certainty, here the *This* is always already a Not-this (a universal, a *That*). More precisely, the instance of discourse is assigned to memory from the very beginning, in such as way, however, that the memorable is the very ungraspability of the instance of discourse as such (and not simply an instance of discourse determined historically and spatially), serving as a basis for the possibility of its infinite repetition. *In the Leopardian idyll, the "this" points always already beyond the hedgerow, beyond the last horizon, toward an infinity of events of language*. Poetic language takes place in such a way that its advent always already escapes both toward the future and toward the past. The place of poetry is therefore always a place of memory and repetition. This implies that the infinite of the Leopardian idyll is not simply a spatial infinity, but (as is made explicit in lines 11-12) first and foremost a temporal infinity.

From this point of view, any analysis of the idyll's temporal shifters becomes extremely significant. The poem begins with a past, "was ever dear to me." The past—as Benveniste's analysis demonstrates—is determined and understood only in relation to that axial dimension of temporality which is the present instance of discourse. The *was* implies necessarily a reference to the present *this*, but in such a way that the *this* appears as a having-always-already-been; it is infinitely drawn back toward the past. All the other temporal shifters in the idyll are in the present tense; but the *was ever* of the first line signals that the present instance of discourse is, in reality, an already been, a past. The instance of discourse, as the axial dimension of temporality, escapes in the idyll back toward the past, just as it also refers forward toward the future, toward a handing-down and an interminable memory.

If our reading of Leopardi is correct, then *L'infinito* expresses that same experience which we saw was constitutive for philosophy itself; namely, that the taking place of language is unspeakable and ungraspable. The word, taking place in time, comes about in such a way that *its advent necessarily remains unsaid in that which is said*. The interminable space that the *This* opens up for the gaze is a place of superhuman and fearful silence. This can only be shown in reference to the instance of discourse (which, even here, is presented as a voice: ''I find myself comparing to this voice/that infinite silence''); and the same instance of discourse can only be memorized and repeated *ad infinitum*, without thus becoming speakable and attainable (*trovabile*).

The poetic experience of dictation seems, thus, to coincide perfectly with the philosophical experience of language. Poetry contains in fact an element that always already warns whoever listens or repeats a poem that the event of language at stake has already existed and will return an infinite number of times. This element, which functions in a certain way as a super-shifter, is the metrical-musical element. We are accustomed to reading poetry as if the metrical element had no importance from a semantic point of view. Certainly, it is said, metrical-musical structure is essential to a given poem and cannot be altered—but usually we do not know *why* it is so essential or what precisely it says in itself. The generic reference to music is not of any help here, since music, according to a tradition that is still held, is precisely a discourse lacking any logical significance (even if it expresses feelings).

And yet whoever repeats the opening line of *L'infinito*:

Sempre caro mi fu quest'ermo colle

or perhaps this line by Saba:

Nella mia giovanezza ho navigato

can attest that the musical element immediately says something of importance, which we cannot dismiss, as modern criticism does, speaking merely of a ''redundance of the signifier.''

The metrical-musical element demonstrates first of all the verse as a place of memory and a repetition. The verse (*versus*, from *verto*, the act of turning, to return, as opposed to *prorsus*, to proceed directly, as in prose) signals for a reader that these words have always already come to be, that they will return again, and that the instance of the word that takes place in a poem is, for this reason, ungraspable. Through the musical element, poetic language commemorates its own inaccessible originary place and it says the unspeakability of the event of language (*it attains*, that is, *the unattainable*).

Muse is the name the Greeks gave to this experience of the ungraspability of the originary place of the poetic word. In the *Ion* (534d), Plato identifies the essential character of the poetic word as the fact of being an *eurema Moisan*, an "invention of the Muses," so that it necessarily escapes whoever tries to speak it. To utter the poetic word signifies "to be possessed by the Muse" (536b); that is to say, without the mythical image, to experience the alienation of the originary place of the word that is implicit in all human speech. For this reason Plato can present the poetic word and its transmission as a magnetic chain that hangs from the Muses and holds poets, rhapsodizers, and listeners together, suspended in a common exaltation. This, Plato says, is the meaning of the most beautiful song (*to kalliston melos*): to demonstrate that poetic words do not originally belong to people nor are they created by them (*ouk anthropina . . . oude anthropon*, 534e).

Precisely inasmuch as philosophy too experiences the place of language as its supreme problem (the problem of being), Plato correctly identified philosophy as the "supreme music" (*os philosophias . . . ouses megistes mousikes: Phaedo* 61a), and the muse of philosophy as the "true muse" (*tes alethines mouses tes meta logon te kai philosophias; Republic* 548b).

The "confrontation" that has always been under way between poetry and philosophy is, thus, much more than a simple rivalry. Both seek to grasp that original, inaccessible place of the word, which, for speaking man, is the highest stake. But both poetry and philosophy, faithful in this to their musical inspiration, finally *demonstrate* this place as *unattainable*. Philosophy, which is born precisely as an attempt to liberate poetry from its "inspiration," finally manages to grasp the Muse and transform it, as "spirit," into its own subject; but this spirit (*Geist*) is, precisely, the negative (*das Negative*), and the "most beautiful voice" (*kallisten phone, Phaedrus* 259d) that belongs to the Muse of the philosophers, according to Plato, is a voice without sound. (For this reason, perhaps neither poetry nor philosophy, neither *verse* nor *prose*, will ever be able to accomplish their millennial enterprise by themselves. Perhaps only a language in which the pure prose of philosophy would intervene at a certain point to break apart the verse of the poetic word, and in which the verse of poetry would intervene to bend the prose of philosophy into a ring, would be the true human language.)

But is it possible that Leopardi's idyll demonstrates nothing more than that unattainability of the place of language that we already learned to recognize as the specific patrimony of the philosophical tradition? Or perhaps can we detect a turn in the last three lines, where the experience of the infinite and of silence is inverted in something that, although presented in the figure of a ''drowning'' *(naufragio)* is not, however, characterized as negative?

E il naufragar m'è dolce in questo mare.

The shifter ''this'' (*questo*) that opened the passage in the first lines, allowing the ''dear'' and the familiar to sink into the abyss of the ''interminable'' and ''silence,'' now indicates the ''immensity'' itself as the place of a *sweet* drowning. Moreover, the ''sweet'' and the ''this'' (sea) of the final line seem to recall explicitly the ''dear'' and the ''this'' (knoll) of the first line, as if the idyll were now returning to its place of origin. Perhaps we cannot comprehend the experience that the final line presents as a sweet drowning except by returning to the opening:

Sempre caro mi fu quest'ermo colle,

which seems practically to be mirrored at the end.

In our previous reading we concentrated especially on the indicators of the utterance (*this* and *was*) and left out the very word that opens the poem: *sempre* (always). In truth, even this adverb contains an element that might be traced back to the sphere of pronouns and so to the sphere of the utterance; the Latin *semper* can be broken down into *sem-per*, where *sem* is the ancient Indo-European term for unity (cf. Greek *eis, en*; the other Indo-European languages substituted another word signifying ''only, single,'' as in the Latin *unus*). *Sempre* (always) signifies *once and for all*, and thus it contains the idea of a unity that intersects and unites a plurality and a repetition. The *sempre* that opens the idyll thus points toward a habit, a *having (habitus)* that unifies (*once*) a multiplicity (*all times*): *the having ever dear this knoll*. The whole idyll can be read in this sense as an attempt to seize a habit (that habit, that ''faculty for getting accustomed to'' that Leopardi describes many times in the *Zibaldone* as the fundamental faculty of man), to experience the meaning of the word *always*. The object of the habit is a ''this,'' that is, as we saw, something that refers to an event of language. But which particular experience of the ''this,'' of the taking place of language, is implicit in the habit, in the having-ever-dear? It is the attempt to respond to this question, that is, to experience the *always*, that jolts the poet into the interminable space ''until my heart/almost becomes dismayed.'' The habit—that which links together—is fragmented into a *this* and a *that,* which mirror each other infinitely: once and then again, interminably, against the *once and for all* of the initial ''always.''

The experience at stake in the idyll is thus the breaking apart of a habit, the rupturing of a habitual dwelling into a "surprise"; the most simple and familiar thing appears suddenly as unattainable and estranged. Habit cedes to a *thought* that "feigns"; that is, it represents the initial *sempre* as an interminable multiplicity. This thought enacts a "comparison" between a *that* and a *this*, "that infinite silence" and "this voice"; that is, between an experience of the place of language as ungraspable immensity (which, later, will appear as a past, "the dead seasons"), and the voice that indicates this very place as something alive and present. The thought is the movement that, fully experiencing the unattainability of the place of language, seeks to *think*, to hold this unattainability in suspense, to measure its dimensions.

On August 8, 1817, Leopardi writes to Giordani:

> Another thing that makes me unhappy is thought. . . . Thought has given me such suffering for so long now, it has always held me entirely at its mercy. . . . It has evidently condemned me, and it will kill me if I do not do something to change my situation.

Years later, at some point before 1831, Leopardi composed a verse with the title *The Domineering Thought (Il pensiero dominante)*. Here thought still holds the poet prisoner, it is his "powerful dominator"; yet it no longer seems like the cause of any unhappiness, but rather it is "very sweet"; a "terrible, but dear/gift from heaven"; reason for worry, certainly, but the "pleasing cause of infinite worries." In the eyes of the poet thought reveals, as in a "stupendous enchantment," a "new immensity"; but this immensity is the sweetest thing, a "paradise." Now thought is "my" thought, the possession that only death will be able to remove from the poet. Thus the powerful dominator has become something to *have*: "what more sweet than the having of your thought," as the last line of the poem reads.

What happened between the letter of 1817 and the moment at which the poet composed *Il pensiero dominante*? What transformed the terrible prism of thought into the sweetest and most personal experience?

We should read a similar reversal, a similar "changing of condition" ("it will kill me if I do not do something to change my situation") in the idyll *L'infinito*. The reversal, through which thought is transformed from a cruel master into a sweet possession, takes the figure of drowning in the idyll. This "sweet" drowning of thought takes place in a "this" that now indicates the same "immensity" disclosed in the place of language at the beginning of the idyll by the rupturing of habit. Thought drowns in that about which it thinks: the unattainable taking place of language. But the drowning of thought in "this" sea now permits a return to the "ever dear" of the first line, the habitual dwelling with which the idyll began. The voyage completed in the "little poem" of *L'infinito* (idyll means "little form") is truly more brief than any time or measure, because it leads into the heart of the Same. It departs from a habit and returns to the same habit. But in this voyage the experience of the event of the word, which opened its unheard silence and interminable spaces in thought, ceases to be a negative experience. The place of language is now truly lost forever *(per sempre)*; forever, that is, once and for all. In its drowning, thought compared, that is, led back toward the Same, the negative dimensions of the event of language, its having-been and its coming to be, its silence and its voice, being and nothingness; and in the extinguishing of thought, in the exhaustion of the dimension of *being*, the figure of humanity's *having* emerges for the first time in its simple clarity: *to have always dear* as one's habitual dwelling place, as the *ethos* of humanity.

Note

1. When Aristotle formulates his table of categories, of the possible *legomena,* what does he say, if not precisely that certain possibilities of speech are already, originally given? Certainly it is possible to demonstrate, as Benveniste has done (1, pp. 63-74), that the Aristotelian categories correspond to parallel structures in Greek (and so they are categories of language before they are categories of thought); but isn't this precisely what Aristotle says, when he presents a table of the possibilities of speech? Here, the error lies in presupposing that the modern concept of language is already formed, when rather, it was constructed historically through a slow process. The Aristotelian table constitutes a fundamental moment in this process.

Excursus 6 (between the seventh and eighth days)

*The essential pertinence of nothingness and of negativity to language and temporality was clearly expressed in a passage from a manuscript by Leonardo (*Cod. Arundel, f. 131r*) that serves as a standard for any theory of negativity.*

> *Among the magnitude of things that are around us, the being of nothingness holds the highest position and its grasp extends to things that have no being, and its essence resides within time, within the past and the future, and it possesses nothing of the present.*

Another fragment from the same folio contains a different version beginning:

> *That which is called nothing is found only in time and in words.*

The being of nothingness, inasmuch as it belongs to time and language, is conceived here as a fundamental greatness ("it holds the highest position"). Moreover, logico-temporal entities (those "things that have no being") are placed in opposition to natural entities, since, having no place in natural entities, they are grounded in and contained by nothingness:

> *Within us nothingness contains all the things that have no being; within time it resides in the past and the future and possesses nothing of the present; and within nature it has no place. (f. 132v)*

The other notes on the folio contain various reflections on the concepts of point, line, and surface, and they demonstrate the strict, operative connection—

which we should never forget—between nothingness and the fundamental geometrical-mathematical concepts.

The Eighth Day

Let us take a moment to look back at the path we have traveled. Beginning with the experience of Da-Sein (Being-the-*there*) in Heidegger, and *das Diese nehmen* (Taking-the-*This*) in Hegel, we saw that both phenomena introduce or "initiate" us into a negativity. This negativity is grounded in the reference that the shifters *Da* and *Diese* make to the pure taking place of language, and distinct from that which, in this taking place, is formulated in linguistic propositions. This dimension—which coincides with the concept of utterance in modern linguistics, but which, throughout the history of metaphysics, has always constituted the field of meaning of the word *being*—finds it final foundation in a Voice. Every shifter is structured like a Voice. However, the Voice presupposed here is defined through a double negativity. On the one hand, it is in fact identified only as a removed voice, as a having-been of the natural *phoné*, and this removal constitutes the originary articulation (*arthron, gramma*) in which the passage from *phoné* to *logos* is carried out, from the living being to language. On the other hand, this Voice cannot be *spoken* by the discourse of which it *shows* the originary taking place. The fact that the originary articulation of language can take place only in a double negativity signifies that language is and is not the voice of man. If language were immediately the voice of man, as braying is the voice of the ass and chirping the voice of the cicada, man could not be-the-*there* or take-the-*this*; that is, he could never experience the taking place of language or the disclosure of being. But if, on the other hand (as demonstrated by both the Heideggerian dialectic of *Stimmung* and *Stimme* and the Hegelian figure of the Voice of death), man radically possessed no voice (not even a negative Voice), every shifter and every possibility of indicating the event of language would disappear equally. A voice—a silent and unspeakable voice—is the supreme shifter, which permits thought to experience the taking place of language and to ground, with it, the dimension of being in its difference with respect to the entity.

As it enacts the originary articulation of *phoné* and *logos* through this double negativity, the dimension of the Voice constitutes the model according to which Western culture construes one of its own supreme problems: the relation and passage between nature and culture, between *phusis* and *logos*. This passage is always already conceived as an *arthron*, an articulation; or rather, as a discontinuity that is also a continuity, a removal that is also a preservation (*arthron*, like *armonia,* originally derives from the language of woodworking; *armotto* signifies to conjoin, to unite, as the woodworker does with two pieces of wood). In this sense, the Voice is truly the invisible *harmony*, which Heraclitus said was stronger than visible harmony (*armonie aphanes phaneres kreitton*; fr. 54 Diels), because in its double negativity, it enacts the conjoinment that constitutes the essence of that *zoon logou echon* that is man. In this definition, the *echein*, the *having,* of man, which unifies the duality of the living being and language, is conceived of as always already existing in the negative mode of an *arthron*. Man is that living being who removes himself and preserves himself at the same time—as unspeakable—in language; negativity is the human means of *having* language. (When Hegel conceives of the negative as *Aufhebung*, he is thinking of the *arthron* as this invisible unification, which is stronger than the visible one because it constitutes the most intimate vital pulsation—*Lebenpuls*—of every existing being.)

The mythogeme of the Voice is, thus, the original mythogeme of metaphysics; but inasmuch as the Voice is also the originary place of negativity, negativity is inseparable from metaphysics. (Here the limitations of all critiques of metaphysics are made evident; they hope to surpass the horizon of metaphysics by radicalizing the problem of negativity and ungroundedness, as if a pure and simple repetition of its *fundamental* problem could lead to a surpassing of metaphysics.)

Inasmuch as the experience of the language of metaphysics has its final, negative foundation in a Voice, this experience is always already divided into two distinct planes. The first, which can only be *shown*, corresponds to the very taking place of language disclosed by the Voice; the second is, on the other hand, the plane of meaningful discourse. It corresponds to what is said within this taking place.

The scission of language into two irreducible planes permeates all of Western thought, from the Aristotelian opposition between the first *ousia* and the other categories (followed by the opposition between *ars inveniendi* and *ars iudicandi*, between topics and logic, which profoundly marks the Greco-Roman experience of language), up to the duality between *Sage* and *Sprache* in Heidegger or between *showing* and *telling* in Wittgenstein. The very structure of transcendence, which constitutes the decisive character of philosophical reflection on being, is grounded in this scission. Only because the event of language always already transcends what is said in this event, can something like a transcendence in the ontological sense be demonstrated.

Even modern linguistics expresses this scission in the unbridgeable opposition between *langue* and *parole* (as demonstrated by the reflection of Saussure's final works, as well as that of Benveniste concerning the double significance of human language). The negative dimension, which constitutes the only possible shifter between these two planes (whose place we have already traced in the history of philosophy as that of the Voice), is present even in modern linguistics within the concept of the *phoneme*, this purely negative and insignificant particle that opens up and makes possible both signification and discourse. But precisely because it constitutes the negative foundation of language, the problem of the *place* of the phoneme cannot be resolved within the context of the science of language. In a kind of serious joke, Jakobson correctly ascribed this problem to ontology: as the "sound of language," in the sense of *langue* (that is, of something that, by definition, cannot have sound), the phoneme is singularly close to the Heideggerian idea of a "Voice without sound" and of a "sound of silence"; and phonology, defined as the science of the sounds of language (*langue*), is a perfect analogue to ontology, which, on the grounds of previous considerations, we can define as the "science of the removed voice, that is, of Voice."

If we now return to our initial point of departure, to that "essential relationship" between language and death that "flashes up before us, but remains still unthought," and that we thus proposed to interrogate, we may now attempt a preliminary response. The essential relationship between language and death takes place—for metaphysics—in Voice. *Death and Voice have the same negative structure and they are metaphysically inseparable*. To experience death as death signifies, in fact, to experience the removal of the voice and the appearance, *in its place*, of another Voice (presented in grammatical thought as *gramma*, in Hegel as the Voice of death, in Heidegger as the Voice of conscience and the Voice of being, and in linguistics as a phoneme), which constitutes the originary *negative* foundation of the human word. To experience Voice signifies, on the other hand, to become capable of another death—no longer simply a deceasing, but a person's ownmost and insuperable possibility, the possibility of his *freedom*.

Here logic shows—within the horizon of metaphysics—its originary and decisive connection with ethics. In fact, in its essence Voice is will or pure meaning (*voler-dire*). The meaning at stake in Voice should not, however, be understood in a psychological sense; it is not something like an impulse, nor does it indicate the volition of a subject regarding a determinate object. The Voice, as we know, says nothing; it does not mean or want to say any significant proposition. Rather, it indicates and means the pure taking place of language, and it is, as such, a purely *logical* dimension. But what is at stake in this will, such that it is able to disclose to man the marvel of being and the terror of nothingness? The Voice does not will any proposition or event; it wills *that language exist*, it wills *the originary event* that contains the possibility of every event. The Voice is the originary ethical dimension in which man pronounces his "yes" to language and consents that it may take place. To consent to (or refuse) language does not here signify simply to speak (or be silent). To consent to language signifies to act in such a way that, in the abysmal experience of the taking place of language, in the removal of the voice, another Voice is disclosed to man, and along with this are also disclosed the dimension of being and the mortal risk of nothingness. To consent to the taking place of language, to listen to the Voice, signifies, thus, to consent also to death, to be capable of dying (*sterben*) rather than simply deceasing (*ableben*).

For this reason, the Voice, the originary *logical* element, is also, for metaphysics, the originary *ethical* element: freedom, the *other* voice, and the *other* death—the Voice of death, we might say to express the unity of their articulation—that makes language *our* language and the world *our* world and constitutes, for man, the negative foundation of his *free* and *speaking* being. Within the horizon of metaphysics, the problem of being is not, finally, separable from that of will, just as logic is not separable from ethics.

The location of the ethical-political problem in the passage from *phoné* to *logos* in Aristotle's *Politics* arises from this originary and insuperable connection:

> Man alone of the animals possesses language (*logos*).The mere voice (*phoné*), it is true, can indicate pain or pleasure, and therefore it is possessed by the other animals as well (for their nature has been developed so far as to have sensations of what is painful and pleasant and to signify these sensations to one another), but language (*logos*) is designed to indicate the advantageous and the harmful, and therefore also the right and wrong; for it is the special property of man in distinction from the other animals that he alone has perception of good and bad and right and wrong and the other moral qualities, and it is partnership in these things that makes a household and a city-state. (1253a, 10-18; English ed., trans. H. Rackham. Cambridge, Mass., 1977)

Similarly, this originary connection is also the source, in the *Critique of Practical Reason*, for the characterization of ethical will as "pure practical *reason*," and in Schelling's *Philosophical Research on the Essence of Human Liberty*, for the presentation of being in its abysmal state as will ("In the final and supreme instance there is no other being but will. Will is the originary being [*Ursein*] and the predicates of this adapt to will alone: absence of foundation, eternity, independence from time, auto-sentimentality. All of philosophy seeks only to find this supreme expression"), and for this will, in turn, as a will that wants nothing.

Only when, on the horizon of metaphysics, the decisive connection between logic and ethics expressed in these three texts has been thought fully, down to its foundation—that is, down to the ungroundedness from which the soundless voice of *Sigé* calls out—will it be possible, if it is indeed possible, to think beyond this horizon, that is beyond Voice and its negativity. In fact, for metaphysics, the common foundation of logic and ethics lies on a negative foundation. For this reason, any understanding of logic must necessarily address an ethical problem that finally remains informulable (Wittgenstein's thought clearly demonstrates this); and in the same way, on the horizon of metaphysics, ethics—which enacts the experience merely shown by logic—must finally address a logical problem, that is, an impossibility of speaking. *The originary unity between logic and ethics is, for metaphysics, sigetics.*

If the relationship between language and death "remains still unthought," it is because the Voice—which constitutes the possibility of this relationship—is the unthinkable on which metaphysics bases every possibility of thought, the unspeakable on which it bases its whole speakability. Metaphysics is the *thought and will of being*, that is, *the thought and will of the Voice* (or thought and will of death); but this "thought" and this "will" must necessarily remain unthematized, because they can only be thematized in terms of the most extreme negativity.[1]

It is here that the Western philosophical tradition shows its originary link with tragic experience. From the dawn of Greek thought, the human experience of language (that is, the experience of the human as both *living and speaking*, a natural being and a logical being) has appeared in the tragic spectacle divided by an unresolvable conflict. In the *Oresteia*, this conflict manifests itself as a contrast between the voice of blood, expressed in the song of the Erinnys (this "funerary song without lyre" (*aneu luras . . . threnon*) which the heart "has learned by itself" (*autodidaktos*), as opposed to the language that it learned from others; *Agamemnon*, vv. 990-93), and the *logos*, the word that discusses and persuades, personified by Athena and by Zeus Agoraios, Zeus of the word that is freely exchanged in public. The reconciliation between these two "voices," each one presented as a right (*dike*) and a destiny (*moira*), is certainly, according to the traditional interpretation, the theme of the Aeschylean trilogy. It is, however, significant that the hero cannot fully recognize himself in either of these voices and that the contrast between the voices gives rise to the properly tragic dimension as an impossibility of speaking:

Ei de me tetagmena
moira moiran ek theon
eirge me pleon pherein,
prophthasasa kardia
glossan an tad exechei

> [If the *moira* assigned by the Gods did not impede *moira* from conveying something more, my heart would go beyond my tongue and utter such things.] (*Agam.*, vv. 1025-29)

It is in this silent *non liquet*, rather than in a positive reconciliation, that we should see, according to the profound intuitions of Rosenzweig and Benjamin, the essence of tragic dialogue. ("Tragedy," writes Rosenzweig, "created the form of the dialogue in order to be able to represent silence.") If there is a reconciliation between the two *"moiras"* of man, between *psusis* and *logos*, between his voice and his language, it can only consist in silence. (Here perhaps we should see the origin of the accusation that, in his tragedies, Aeschylus revealed the Eleusinian mysteries; cf. Aristotle, *Nicomachean Ethics* IIIIa.)

In Sophocles' *Oedipus the King*, the division, always already inherent in every human word, appears most clearly. As a *living being* who has *language*, man is subjected to a double destiny. He cannot *know* all that he says and if *he wills* to know, he is subjected to the possibility of error and *hubris*. Now language becomes the site of a conflict between that which one can consciously know in any utterance and that which one necessarily says without knowing. Destiny is presented precisely as that part of language that man, because of his double *moira*, cannot be conscious of. So, at the moment when he is moved by the will to "investigate every word" (*panta gar skopo logon*, v. 291), Oedipus believes that he is affirming his own innocence and the limit of his own conscious "knowing with himself" (*suneidenai*). Instead, it is precisely then that he speaks own condemnation:

> Ekeuchomai d', oikosin ei xunestios
> en tois emois genoit emou xuneidotos,
> pathein aper toisd' artios erasamen.

> [For myself, I wish that if the killer were a guest in my house and I was aware of it (*xuneidotos*), I might endure the pain of that same curse that I just cast onto the others.] (vv. 249-51)

Believing that he has solved the enigma of language and has thus discovered a "technique which goes beyond every technique" (*techne technes uperpherousa*; v. 380), he finally confronts the enigma of his own birth, of his own *phusis*, and he succumbs to it. In the words of the chorus in *Oedipus at Colonus* we can find the quintessence of the tragic experience of language:

> Me phunai ton apanta ni-
> ka logon to d', epei phane,
> benai keithen othen per e-
> kei, polu deuteron, os tachista.

[Not being born overcomes all language; but, having come into the light, the best thing is to return as soon as possible whence one came.] (vv. 1224-27)

Only *me phunai*, not being born, not having a nature (*phusis*), can overcome language and permit man to free himself from the guilt that is built up in the link of destiny between *phusis* and *logos*, between life and language. But since this is precisely impossible, since man is *born* (he has both a birth and nature), the best thing is for him to return as soon as possible whence he came, to ascend beyond his birth through the silent experience of death. (In the previous verses, death is defined as "without songs, without a lyre, without dance," "*anumenaios, aluros, achoros.*")

Philosophy, in its search for another voice and another death, is presented, precisely, as both a return to and a surpassing of tragic knowledge; it seeks to grant a voice to the silent experience of the tragic hero and to constitute this voice as a foundation for man's most proper dimension.

It is within this context that we should examine the appearance of the theme of *suneidesis* (*con-science*) in the tragedians. The term *suneidesis* (like the related *sunnoia*) indicates a "knowing with oneself" (*suneidenai eauto* is the expression found in Sophocles, Euripides, and Aristophanes, and even earlier in Sappho), which always has an ethical connotation, inasmuch as, in general, it has for its object guilt (or innocence) and is accompanied by *pathos*:

Ti chrema pascheis; tis s' apollusin nosos;
'H sunesis, oti sunoida dein' eirgasmenos.

[What are you suffering from? What evil destroys you?—Conscience, because I am conscious (with myself) of having done something terrible.] (Euripides, *Oresteia,* vv. 395-96)

But it is important that this consciousness (Knowing-with-oneself)—which, as such, necessarily implies a reference to the sphere of *logos*—appears, rather, as mute, and is manifested in a terrible silence. In the *Eunomia* of Solon, one of the oldest documents containing the verb *suneidenai*, the *ethical* and *silent* character of this consciousness (here referring to Dike itself) is already present:

E sigosa sunoide ta gignomena pro t' eonta, to de chrone pantos elth apoteisamene.

[By remaining silent [Dike] knows-with-itself things past and, at the right moment, it intervenes in every case to punish.]

And, in Aeschylus's *Prometheus Bound*, the *sunnoia* of the hero is revealed as a silent experience that "devours the heart":

Me toi chlide dokeite med' authadia
sigan me sunnoia de daptomai kear,
oron emauton ode prouseloumenon.

[Do not suppose that I am silent out of pride or arrogance; it is because of the consciousness which devours my heart, seeing myself so mistreated.] (vv. 436-38)

Silence is so essential to this consciousness (knowing-with) that it is often attributed to an inanimate object (in Sophocles' *Philoctetes*, vv. 1081-85, the rocky cave where the hero lies down is conscious along with him; in *Electra*, vv. 92-95, the "sleepless bed" consciously shares pain with the heroine). When it is too rashly translated into words, as in the verses from *Oedipus* cited above, silence opens the passage from which *hubris* threatens to emerge. The definition of conscience (*sunnoia*) that we find in one of the Platonic *oroi* is perfectly consistent with these tragic passages: *dianoia meta lupes aneu logou*, "thought with pain without discourse" (which, if we think carefully, is almost the same description that Heidegger offers for the Voice of conscience).

It is this mute and anguished conscience, this *sigetics* opened between the being-born of man and his speaking being, which philosophy, following the most profound demand of the tragic spectacle, posits as the foundation for both logic and ethics. This is not the place to follow the development of the concept of *suneidesis* in post-tragic Greek thought; nor to demonstrate how, already in Socrates, this became a "demonic" element and acquired a voice (*daimonion[ti], phoné tis, Apology* 31d); nor how, in the Stoa, expressed as "right conscience" (*orthe suneidesis*), it came to represent supreme certainty for mankind. It is important to observe here how the "conscience" of Western philosophy rests originally on a mute foundation (a Voice), and it will never be able to fully resolve this silence. By rigorously establishing the limits of that which can be known in what is said, logic takes up this silent Voice and transforms it into the negative foundation of all knowledge. On the other hand, ethics experiences it as that which must necessarily remain unsaid in what is said. In both cases, however, the final foundation remains rigorously informulable.

If this Voice is the mystical foundation for our entire culture (its logic as well as its ethics, its theology as well as its politics, its wisdom as well as its madness) then the mystical is not something that can provide the foundation for another thought—attempting to think beyond the horizon of metaphysics, at the extreme confine of which, at the point of nihilism, we are still moving. The mystical is nothing but the unspeakable foundation; that is, the negative foundation of ontotheology. Only a liquidation of the mystical can open up the field to a thought (or language) that thinks (speaks) beyond the Voice and its *sigetics*; that dwells, that is, not on an unspeakable foundation, but in the infancy *(in-fari)* of man.

Perhaps the age of absolutely speakable things, whose extreme nihilistic furor we are experiencing today, the age in which all the figures of the Unspeakable and all the masks of ontotheology have been *liquidated*, or released and spent in words that now merely show the nothingness of their foundation; the age in which all human experience of language has been redirected to the final negative reality of a willing that means (*vuole-dire*) nothing—perhaps this age is also the age of man's in-fantile dwelling (in-fantile, that is, without Voice or will, and yet *ethical*, habitual) in language.

Is there an attempt within metaphysics to think its own unthinkable, to grasp, that is, the negative foundation itself? We saw that the originary disclosure of language, its taking place, which discloses to man both being and freedom, cannot be expressed in language. Only the Voice with its marvelous muteness shows its inaccessibile place, and so the ultimate task of philosophy is necessarily to think the Voice. Inasmuch as the Voice is, however, that which always already divides every experience of language and structures the original difference between showing and telling, being and entity, world and thing, then to grasp the Voice can only signify to think beyond these oppositions; that is, to think *the Absolute*. The Absolute is the mode in which philosophy thinks its own negative foundation. In the history of philosophy, it receives various names: *idea tou agathou* in Plato, *theoria, noeseos noesis* in Aristotle, *One* in Plotinus, *Indifference* in Schelling, *Absolute Idea* in Hegel, *Ereignis* in Heidegger; but in every case, the Absolute has the structure of a process, of an exit from itself that must cross over negativity and scission in order to return to its own place.

The verb *to solve*, from which the term "absolute" derives, can be broken down into *se-luo*. In the Indo-European languages, the reflexive group **se* indicates what is proper (*suus*)—both that which belongs to a group, in the sense of *con-suetudo, suesco* (Gr. *ethos*, "custom, habit," Ger. *Sitte*), and that which remains in itself, separated, as in *solus, sed, secedo*. The verb *to solve* thus indicates the operation of dissolving (*luo*) that leads (or leads back) something to its own **se*, to *suus* as to *solus*, dissolving it—*absolving it*—of every tie or alterity. The preposition *ab*, which expresses distancing, movement from, reinforces this idea of a process, a voyage that takes off, separates from something and moves, or returns toward something.

To think the Absolute signifies, thus, to think that which, through a process of "absolution," has been led back to its ownmost property, to itself, to its own *solitude*, as to its own *custom*. For this reason, the Absolute always implies a voyage, an abandonment of the originary place, an alienation and a being-outside. If the Absolute is the supreme idea of philosophy, then philosophy is truly, in the words of Novalis, nostalgia (*Heimweh);* that is, the "desire to be at home everywhere" (*Trieb überall zu Hause zu sein*), to recognize oneself in being-other. Philosophy is not initially at home, it is not originally in possession of itself, and thus it must return to itself. When Hegel thinks of the Absolute as a result (*Resultat*), he simply thinks fully the very essence of the Absolute. Inasmuch as this implies a process of "absolution," an experience and a return, it is always a result; only at the end does it reach where it was in the beginning.

The word, which wants to grasp the Voice as Absolute, which wants, that is, *to be* in its own originary place, must already be outside of it, and must assume and recognize the nothingness that is in the voice. Crossing over time and the scission that reveals itself in the place of language, the word must return to itself and, absolving itself of this scission, it must be at the end there where, without knowing it, it was already in the beginning; that is, in the Voice.

Philosophy is this voyage, the human word's *nostos* (return) from itself to itself, which, abandoning its own habitual dwelling place in the voice, opens itself to the terror of nothingness and, at the same time, to the marvel of being; and after becoming meaningful discourse, it returns in the end, as *absolute* wisdom, to the Voice. Only in this way can thought finally be at home and "absolved" of the scission that threatened it from there where it always already was. Only in the Absolute can the word, which experienced "homesickness" (*Heimweh*) and the "pain of return" (*nost-algia*), which experienced the negative always already reigning in its habitual dwelling place, now truly reach its own beginning in the Voice.

The Greek term for "habitual dwelling place," or "habit," is *ethos*. The *ethos* of humanity is thus, for philosophy, always already divided and threatened by a negative. One of the oldest testimonies of a philosophical reflection on *ethos* characterizes the habitual dwelling of humanity with these words:

ethos anthropo daimon (Heraclitus, fr. 119 Diels).

Daimon does not simply denote here a divine figure. Its etymology leads back to the verb *daiomai*, to lacerate, to divide, so *daimon* signifies the lacerator, he who cuts and divides.

The fragment from Heraclitus should thus be translated: "*Ethos*, the habitual dwelling place of man, is that which lacerates and divides." Habit, the dwelling in which one always already exists, is the place of scission; it is that which one can never grasp without receiving a laceration and a division, the place where one can never really be *from the beginning*, but can only return to *at the end*. It is this demonic scission, this *daimon* that threatens humans in the very core of their *ethos*, of their habitual dwelling place, that philosophy has always to think, and to "absolve." For this reason philosophy must necessarily have its beginning in "marvel," it must, that is, always already leave behind its habit, always already alienate itself and divide itself from its habit, in order to be able to return there, walking through negativity and absolving it from its demonic scission. A philosopher is one who, having been surprised by language, having thus abandoned his habitual dwelling place in the word, must now return to where language already happened to him. He must "surprise the surprise," be at home in the marvel and in the division. When it wishes to return to its *arche*, philosophy can only grasp the taking place of language in a Voice, in a negative; that is, the *daimon* itself as *ethos*, the scission itself as the appearance (*Erscheinung*) of the Absolute. That which it has to grasp is, after all, simply a dispossession and a flight.

But—let us now ask—do the Voice and its negativity really do justice to the *ethos* of man? If the return is the supreme problem of philosophy, what is there to which it must, in the end, return?

The verb *to return* derives from the Greek *tornios* (lathe); that is, from the name of the simple woodworking instrument that, turning around on itself, uses and consumes the object it forms until it has reduced the material to a perfect circle. (*Tornios* belongs to the same root as the Greek *teiro*, use, like the Latin verb *tero* and the English adjective *trite*.) How should we conceive, then, this turning on itself, this circular rotation of being and truth? To what does the human word return? Only to what has already been? And if that which has always already been is, in the words of Hegel, a non-being (*gewesen ist kein Wesen*), then won't *ethos*, the habitual dwelling place of humanity to which the word returns, necessarily lie beyond being and its Voice?

Is it possible that *being* (ontotheology with its component negativity) is not up to the level of the simple mystery of humans' *having*, of their *habitations* or their *habits*? And what if the dwelling to which we return beyond being were neither a supercelestial place nor a Voice, but simply the *trite* words that we *have*?

Now, having reached the end of our research, which brought us to identify the originary mythogeme of metaphysics in the silence of the Voice, we can begin to read a text in which Nietzsche seems to want to stage the end of philosophy and the beginning of its "posterity" in a brief tragic monologue. Oedipus, the tragic hero par excellence, is presented here as the "last philosopher." In a fragment from 1872 titled *Ödipus* and subtitled, *Reden des letzten Philosophen mit sich selbst. Ein Fragment aus der Geschichte der Nachwelt,* we read:

> I am called the last philosopher because I am the last man. No one speaks to me except me myself, and my voice reaches me like that of a dying man. With you, lovely voice, with you, last breath of a memory of all human happiness, let me be with you for just one more hour; through you I trick solitude and I let myself be deluded in multiplicity and love, because my heart refuses to believe that love is dead; it cannot sustain the shiver of the most solitary of solitudes and it forces me to speak as if I were two.
>
> Do you still hear me, my voice? Do you murmur a curse? If only your curse could break up the viscera of this world! But the world still lives, and alone it watches me, full of splendor and ever colder with its

> pitiless stars. It is alive, stupid and blind as always, and only *one* dies—man.
>
> And yet! I am still listening to you, lovely voice! Another beyond me also dies, the last man, in this universe: the last breath, *your* breath dies with me, the long Oh! Oh! breathed down on me, the last man of pain, Oedipus.

Even in this text, the experience of death and the experience of the Voice are tightly linked. In death, Oedipus, the last philosopher, discovers the "most solitary of solitudes." He is absolutely alone in language before the world and nature ("no one speaks to me, except me myself"); and, even here, in this extreme negativity, man retrieves a Voice, a "final breath of memory," which returns his past to him and intervenes to save him from solitude, forcing him to speak.

Philosophy is this dialogue between man—the *speaking* and *mortal* being—and his Voice; this strenuous search for the Voice—and, with it, a memory—facing death, assuring language of its place. The Voice is the mute ethical companion running to the aid of language at the point where it reveals its ungroundedness. By remaining silent, with its "breath," it assumes this absence of foundation and makes room for it.

In the soliloquy of Oedipus, however, the Voice is finally only an impotent "curse" and an illusion that, as such, must also die. Many years later, in a fragment from 1886 to 1887, Nietzsche seems to respond to the illusion of the last philosopher in a context where the philosopher no longer hears any Voice and where every tie with the figure of the living has been severed. Nietzsche writes:

> Not to hear any response after such an appeal to the depths of the soul—no voice in response—is a terrible experience which could destroy the most hardened man: in me it has severed all ties with living men.

With the definitive death of the Voice, even philosophy—the soliloquy of Oedipus—must come to an end. Thought, which thinks after the end of philosophy, cannot still be the thought of the Voice, of the taking place of language in the Voice; nor can it be the thought of the death of the Voice. Only if the human voice is not simply death, but has never existed, only if language no longer refers to any Voice (and, thus, not even to a *gramma*, that is, to a removed voice), is it possible for man to experience a language that is not marked by negativity and death.

What is a language without Voice, a word that is not grounded in any meaning? This is something that we must still learn to think. But with the disappearance of the Voice, that "essential relation" between language and death that dominates the history of metaphysics must also disappear. Man, as a speaking being, is no longer necessarily the mortal, he who has the "faculty for death" and is reaffirmed by death; nor, as a dying being, is he necessarily the speaker, he who has the "faculty for language" and is reaffirmed by this. To exist in language without being called there by any Voice, simply to die without being called by death, is, perhaps, the most abysmal experience; but this is precisely, for man, also his most *habitual* experience, his *ethos*, his dwelling, always already presented in the history of metaphysics as demonically divided into the living and language, nature and culture, ethics and logic, and therefore only attainable in the negative articulation of a Voice. And perhaps only beginning with the eclipse of the Voice, with the no longer taking place of language and with the death of the Voice, does it become possible for man to experience an *ethos* that is no longer simply a *sigetics*. Perhaps man—the animal who seems not to be encumbered by any specific nature or any specific identity—must experience his poverty even more radically. Perhaps humans are even poorer than they supposed in attributing to themselves the experience of negativity and death as their specific anthropogenetic patrimony, and in basing every community and tradition on this experience.

At the end of *Oedipus at Colonus*, when the now-serene hero reaches the hour of death, he begs Theseus, who has accompanied him in those final instants, that no mortal should "utter a voice" at his tomb (*met' epiphonein medena thneton/ theken*, vv. 1762-63). If Theseus will respect this vow, he will have "a country forever without pain" (*choran . . . aien alupon*, v. 1765). By breaking the link between language and death, Oedipus—"the last man of pain"—puts an end to the chain of tragic guilt that is interminably transmitted in the nexus between the two *moiras* of man.

According to the teaching of tragic wisdom, this separation can only take place in death; and yet here, no voice is heard in death, not even the silent Voice of the tragic conscience. Rather, a "country forever without pain" is revealed to humanity, while, beyond the lament, the figure of a "having" that definitely upholds the entire history in its domain is traced:

> All' apopauete med' epi pleio
> threnon egeirete
> pantos gar echei tade kuros
>
> [But cease now from lamenting: in fact a
> having holds these things entirely.]

This *chora*, this country without pain where no voice is spoken at death, is perhaps that which, beyond the Voice, remains to be thought as the most human dimension, the only place where something like a *me phunai* is possible for man, a not having been born and not having nature. It is this same country that a poem by Paul Klee (a poet who claimed to dwell among the unborn) calls *Elend* (misery; but according to the etymology—cf. *alius*—''another land''):

Land ohne Band,
neues Land,
ohne Hauch
der Erinnerung,
mit dem Rauch
von fremden Herd.
Zügellos!
wo mich trug
keiner Mutter Schoss.

[Land without chains,
new land
without the breath
of memory,
with the smoke
of a strange hearth.
Reinless!
Where I was brought
by no mother's womb.] (Klee, ''1914,'' p. 84)

The geography and the politics of this land, to which man was not brought by any birth and in which he no longer seems mortal, go beyond the limits that we proposed in this seminar. And yet the experience of language expressed here can no longer have the form of a voyage that, separating itself from the proper habitual dwelling place and crossing the marvel of being and the terror of nothingness, returns there where it originally was; rather, here language, as in a verse by one of the great contemporary Italian poets, returns to that which never was and to that which it never left, and thus it takes the simple form of a habit:

Sono tornato là
dove non ero mai stato.
Nulla, da come non fu, è mutato.
Sul tavolo (sull'incerato
a quadretti) ammezzato
ho ritrovato il bicchiere
mai riempito. Tutto
è ancora rimasto quale
mai l'avevo lasciato.

[I returned there
where I have never been.
Nothing has changed from how it was not.
On the table (on the checkered
tablecloth) half-full
I found the glass
which was never filled. All
has remained just as
I never left it.] (Giorgio Caproni, "Ritorno," p. 392)

Note

1. Heidegger 3, p. 215; English ed., pp. 107-8. We hear today that knowledge (in its pure form: as mathematics) has no need of foundation. That is certainly true if, with inadequate representation, we think of foundation as something substantial and positive. But it is no longer true if we conceive of foundation as it is in the history of metaphysics, that is, as an absolute, negative foundation. The Voice (*gramma*, the quantum of signification) remains presupposed in all knowledge and in mathematics. Even if we agree with the possibility of formalizing all mathematics, the possibility of writing, the fact that signs exist, would still remain as a presupposition. "The totality of mathematics today," affirms a well-known French mathematician, "can be written . . . by utilizing only the symbols of logic, without granting that any 'significance' in relation to that which we think." Here the three words "can be written" represent that which remains unthought: this single, unperceived presupposition is precisely the *gramma*. "In the beginning was the sign," according to Hilbert. But, we might object, why is there signification? Why do (pure) signs exist? And we should then respond: "Because there is a will to speak." The final presupposition of all mathematics, the *absolute matheme*, is will or pure meaning *(voler-dire*, nothingness); in the terms of this seminar, the Voice. In theology, this is expressed in the statement that if there were not always already a will in God, He would have remained cloistered in his abyss without expressing any word (the Son). Without will or love, God would have consigned himself to Tartarus, sinking eternally into his own abyss. But, we ask, what would have happened if there were no trace of self in God, no will? If we let God fall headlong into his abyss?

Excursus 7 (after the final day)

If the Voice indicates the taking place of language as time, if thought is that experience of language that, in every proposition and in every phrase, experiences the very taking place of language (that is to say, it thinks being and time in their co-belonging in the Voice), how is it possible to think the Voice in itself, to think absolute time? In the response to this question it is possible to grasp both the proximity of and the diversity between Hegel's Absolute and Heidegger's Ereignis.

At the end of the Jena lessons of 1805-6, Hegel expresses his attitude toward this "thought of time" (Gedanke der Zeit*). The wisdom of philosophy, absolute wisdom, is a "restored immediateness"* (die wiederhergestellte Unmittelbarkeit*), the spirit that, after having left itself, now returns to its own beginning and knows itself absolutely, overcoming the scission that separated it from itself* at the beginning*:*

> *Die Philosophie entäussert sich ihrer selbst, kommt bei ihrem Anfange, dem unmittelbaren Bewusstsein an, das eben das Entzweite ist. Sie ist so Mensch überhaupt; und wie der Punkt des Menschen ist, ist die Welt, und wie sie ist, ist er: ein Schlag erschafft sie beide. Was ist vor dieser Zeit gewesen? das Andre der Zeit, nicht eine andre Zeit, sondern die Ewigkeit, der Gedanke der Zeit. Darin ist die Frage aufgehoben; denn diese meint eine andre Zeit. Aber so ist die Ewigkeit selbst in der Zeit; sie ist ein Vorher der Zeit, also selbst Vergangenheit: es ist gewesen, absolut gewesen: es ist nicht. Die Zeit is der reine Begriff, das angeschaute leere Selbst in seiner Bewegung, wie der Raum in seiner*

> *Ruhe. Vorher, eh[e] die erfüllte Zeit ist, ist die Zeit gar nicht. Ihre Erfüllung ist das Wirkliche, aus der leeren Zeit in sich Zurückgekehrte. Sein Anschauen seiner selbst ist die Zeit, das Ungegenständliche. Wenn wir aber sagen: vor der Welt, [meinen wir:] Zeit ohne Erfüllung. Der Gedanke der Zeit [ist] eben das Denkende, das Insich-Reflektierte. Es ist notwendig, hinauszugehen über diese Zeit, jede Periode, aber in den Gedanken der Zeit: jenes [ist die] schlechte Unendlichkeit, die das nie erreicht, wohinaus sie geht.*
>
> *[Philosophy alienates itself from itself, it arrives at its beginning, at immediate consciousness, which is precisely the scission. This is the case for man in general; and just as the point of man exists, so too the world exists: a blow creates them both. What was there before this time? The other* of time, *not another* time, *but eternity, the thought of time. With that the question is superseded; since this means* another time. *But eternity itself is in time; it is a before time, thus it is itself a past: it was, absolutely was: it is not.* Time *is the pure notion, the empty* itself *intuited in its movement, like space in its rest. Before completed (*erfüllte*) time, time simply does not exist. Its completion is the real, which returns from empty time to itself. Its intuition of itself is time, the Non-objective. If, however, we say:* before *the world, we mean: time without completion. The thought of time is the thinking, the Reflected-in-itself. It is necessary to overcome this time, every period, but in the idea of time; that is the bad infinity, which never reaches its destination.] (Hegel 4, p. 273)*

*For Hegel, then, the desire to think of eternity as a before all time or as another time is impossible, and any thought of time that desires to cross backward across empty time in order to reach the eternal necessarily leads to a bad infinity. Eternity in this sense is nothing other than the past, and as we know, this does not exist. Only completed time is true and real, that which has returned to itself from empty time. For this reason, Hegel says that the Absolute is not the beginning, what is before time, but only the result that has returned to itself. The Absolute is ''only at the end what it truly is.'' It is ''the circle returned on itself which presupposes (*voraussetzt*) its beginning and reaches it only at the end'' (Hegel 2, p. 585). If the Absolute can never be itself at the beginning, it cannot, on the other hand, be identified with the infinite empty course of time. It must necessarily complete time,* finish it. Spirit can grasp itself as absolute only at the end of time. *Hegel affirms this clearly in the final pages of the* Phenomenology*: ''Spirit necessarily appears in time and it appears there until it can grasp its pure concept. . . . Until the spirit is completed in itself, as spirit of the world, it cannot reach its completion as self-conscious spirit'' (*ibid., *pp. 584-85).*

The beginning, which was presupposed as a past and went to the ground like a foundation, can only be reached at the end, when the history to which it gave a beginning (presupposing itself and going to the ground) is definitely completed.

Hence the essential orientation of the Absolute toward the past, and its presentation in the figure of totality and memory. Contrary to an ancient tradition of thought that considers the present as the privileged dimension of temporality, Hegel's past is completed time, time returned unto itself. It is, however, a past that has abolished its essential relation with the present and with the future. It is a "perfect" past, of which Hegel writes—in the text that most thoroughly explores the Bewegung *of time—that it is "the dimension of the totality of time" and "the paralyzed restlessness of the absolute concept" (Hegel 6, p. 204). It is this past, this having-been, which thought has to think as absolved in absolute knowledge. (In the terms of our seminar, we might say that we must absolve the Voice from its having-been, from its being presupposed as removed, and thus we must think Voice and the foundation as absolute.)*

*It is again such a "thought of time" and such a "having-been" that Heidegger begins above all to reclaim as the theme of his thought. In an important passage, he formulates the supreme problem of his own thought in terms of an "advent of the having-been" (*Ankunft des Gewesen*), where "the release of every* it is*" is carried out (*der Abschied von allem "es ist," *Heidegger 3, p. 154). In the "Summary of a Seminar on the Lecture* Zeit und Sein,*" Heidegger enunciates the difference between his thought and Hegel's, affirming that "from Hegel's point of view, one could say:* Sein und Zeit *gets caught in Being; it does not develop Being to the 'concept' " (Heidegger 6, p. 52; English ed., p. 48). That* Gewesen, *that having-been, which introduces negation and the mediation into immediate consciousness in the beginning of the* Phenomenology, *and which for Hegel is only fully realized* at the end, *still remains problematic for Heidegger. However, even here it is not simply a past, but a* Ge-wesen*; that is, the recollection (*ge-*) of that which lasts and exists (*Wesen*). Even here, the beginning is not something simple, but it hides a beginning (*Anfang*) within itself that only a memorial thought (*Andenken*) can reveal.*

Here it is possible to measure the proximity of the Hegelian Absolute to that extreme figure that, in Heidegger, seeks to grasp the advent of the having-been: Ereignis. *According to Heidegger,* Ereignis *seeks to think the co-belonging (*Zusammengehoren*) of Being and time; that is, it interrogates the* und *of the title* Sein und Zeit *(thus, something that cannot be grasped either as Being or as time; Heidegger 6, p. 46). This reciprocal belonging is not, however, simply conceived as a relation between two preexisting entities, but as that which conveys them in their proper existence, like the* Es *that "gives" in the expressions:* es gibt Sein, es gibt Zeit.

How are we to conceive Ereignis *in the context of our seminar? The co-belonging and the interweaving of Being and time have been expressed in terms of the taking place of language in time, that is, as Voice. In* Ereignis, *we might* then say, Heidegger attempts to think the Voice in itself, no longer simply as a mere logico-differential structure and as a purely negative relation of Being and time, but as that which gives and attunes Being and time. In other words, he attempts to conceive the Voice absolved from negativity, the absolute Voice. In Heideggerian language the word Ereignis is semantically related to the word Absolute. In fact, in Ereignis, we should understand the eigen, the ownmost, as in Absolute the self and its own. In this sense, Ereignis might have the same meaning as the Latin "ad-sue-fectio," habituation, absolution. The reciprocal appropriation of Being and time that takes place in Ereignis is, also, a reciprocal absolution that frees them of all relativity and demonstrates their relation as "absolute relation," the "relation of all relations" (das Verhältnis aller Verhältnisse, Heidegger 3, p. 267). For this reason, Heidegger can write that in Ereignis he seeks to think "Being without regard for the entity" (Heidegger 6, p. 25)—that is, in terms of our seminar, the taking place of language without regard for that which, in this taking place, is spoken or formulated as a proposition. This does not mean, Heidegger warns, that "the relation with the entity would be inessential to Being or that it would be necessary to exclude this relation" (ibid., p. 35). Rather, it means "to think Being not in the manner of metaphysics," which considers Being exclusively in its function as the foundation for the entity and thus subordinates being to itself. In fact, metaphysics is "the history of the formations of Being (Seinsprägungen), that is, viewed from Appropriation (Ereignis), of the history of the self-withdrawal of what is sending in favor of the destinies" (ibid., p. 44; English ed., p. 41). In the terms of our seminar, this suggests that, in metaphysics, the taking place of language (the pure fact that language is) is obliterated in favor of that which is said in the instance of discourse; that is, this taking place (the Voice) is thought only as the foundation of the said, in such a way that the Voice itself never truly arrives at thought.

We must now ask if such an absolution and appropriation of the Voice is possible. Is it possible to absolve the Voice from its constitutive negativity and to think the Voice absolutely? Much is determined by the response we give to this question. Yet we can already anticipate that Ereignis does not seem to be entirely liberated from negativity or the unspeakable. "We can never represent Ereignis" (ibid., p. 24); "Ereignis does not exist nor does it present itself"; it is only nameable as a pronoun, as It (Es) and as That (Jenes) "which has sent the various forms of epochal Being," but that, in itself, is "ahistorical, or more precisely, without destiny" (ungeschichtlich, besser: geschicklos; ibid., p. 44; English ed., p. 41).

Even here, as in the Hegelian Absolute, at the point where, in the Ereignis, the sender is revealed as the Proper, the history of Being reaches its end (ist . . . die Seinsgeschichte zu Ende) and, for thought, there is literally nothing left to say or think other than this "appropriation or habit." But in its essence, this amounts to an expropriation (Enteignis) and a hiding (Verbergung), which no longer *hides itself (*sich nicht verbirgt*) and is no longer veiled in historical figures or words, but is shown as such: as pure sending without destiny, pure forgetting of the beginning (Heidegger 6, p. 44). In* Ereignis, *we might say, Voice shows itself as that which, remaining unsaid and unsignified in every word and in every historical tradition, consigns humanity to history and signification as the unspeakable tradition that forms the foundation for all tradition and human speech. Only in this way can metaphysics think* ethos, *the habitual dwelling place of man.*

Here the necessary belonging of self-demonstration to the sphere of the absolute foundation is made clear. In fact, for Hegel the Absolute is not simply the without-relation or the without-movement; rather, it is absolute relation and movement, a complete relation unto itself. Thus, not every significance or every relation to alterity disappears here; but the Absolute is essentially "equal to itself in being-other," "a concept that realizes itself through its being-other and that, through the removal of this reality, is united with itself and reestablishes its absolute reality, its simple self-reference" (Hegel 3, p. 565). That which has returned to itself is not, however, without relation; it is in relation with itself, it shows itself. Signification, which has exhausted its historical figures and no longer signifies nothingness, *now signifies or* shows itself. *Self-demonstration is the absolute relation that does not show or signify other than itself.* The Absolute is the self-demonstration of the Voice.

Here, the link between Ereignis *and the Absolute receives further confirmation. In fact, even in* Ereignis *movement and self-demonstration take place: "the lack of destiny of* Ereignis *does not mean that it has no 'movement' (*Bewegtheit*). Rather, it means that the manner of movement most proper to* Ereignis, *turning toward us in withdrawal, first shows itself as what is to be thought" (Heidegger 3, p. 44). Thus the* Sage, *originary speech, which constitutes "the most authentic mode" of* Ereignis, *is essentially pure self-demonstration,* Zeige *and* sich zeigen *(Heidegger 3, p. 254).*

Further examination of the link (and of the differences) between Ereignis *and the* Absolute *must be deferred until a later date. Such an examination should certainly begin with the problem of completion. If the words Absolute and* Ereignis *have any meaning, this is inseparable from the question of the end of history and tradition. If the Voice is the Insignificant, which goes to the ground so that meaning can be founded, and the beginning, which was presupposed and only came to be replaced in itself at the end, then this Voice can reach meaning only as an end and completion of meaning. The thought of the having-been (of the First) is necessarily a thought of the Last, eschatology.*

*Does the "conclusion" of the Hegelian figures of the spirit in absolute knowing (*hat also der Geist die Bewegung seiner Gestaltens beschlossen, *Hegel 2, p. 588) truly signify the end of history? Kojéve's reading of Hegel, according to which absolute knowing would coincide with a book recapitulating all the historical figures of humanity (and such a book would be identical to the* Science of

Logic*), remains hypothetical. But it is probable that, in the Absolute, the labor of human negativity has truly reached completion and that humanity, returned to itself, ceases to have a human figure to present itself as the fulfilled animality of the species* Homo sapiens, *in a dimension where nature and culture are necessarily confused. (Here, Marx's concept of the human condition as post-historical [or truly historical]—that is, after the end of the reign of necessity and the entrance of the "reign of freedom"—is still a contemporary idea.)*

In Heidegger, the figure of "appropriated" or post-historical humanity remains ambiguous. On the one hand, the fact that the hiding of Being takes place in Ereignis*—but no longer veiled in an epochal figure and thus, without any historical destiny—can only signify that Being is now definitively obliterated and that its history, as Heidegger repeatedly suggests, is finished. On the other hand, Heidegger writes that in* Ereignis *some possibilities of unveiling remain that thought cannot exhaust and, thus, there are still some historical destinies (*Schickungen, *Heidegger 6, p. 53). Moreover, man still seems here to maintain the status of the speaking-mortal. Rather,* Ereignis *is precisely the movement that carries language as* Sage *to human speech (Heidegger 3, p. 261). In this sense, "All proper (*eigentlich*) language—as assigned to man through the movement of the* Sage*—is destined (*geschickt*) and thus, destinal (*geschicklick*)" (Heidegger 3, p. 264). Human language, no longer linked to any nature, remains destined and historical.*

Since both the Absolute and Ereignis *are oriented toward a having-been or* Gewesen *of which they represent the consummation, the lineaments of a truly absolved, truly appropriated humanity—one that is wholly without destiny—remain in both cases obscure.*

(So if we wished to characterize the perspective of the seminar with respect to the having-been in Hegel and in Heidegger, we could say that thought is oriented here in the direction of a never-having-been. *This is to say that our seminar sets out from the definitive cancellation of the Voice; or rather, it conceives of the Voice as never having been, and it no longer thinks the Voice, the unspeakable tradition. Its place is the* ethos, *the infantile dwelling—that is to say, without will or Voice—of man in language. This dwelling, which has the figure of a history and of a universal language that have never been and are thus no longer destined to be handed down in a grammar, is that which remains here, to be thought. It is in this context that we should read the poem by Caproni that ended the seminar.)*

A final thing remains to be said regarding the Eleusinian mystery. We saw that its simple wisdom, initiating man to negation and to the "mystery of eating bread and drinking wine," was central to the Phenomenology of Spirit. *How should we understand the solidarity between philosophy and the mysterious wisdom evoked here? And what is meant by this proximity between unspeakable sacrificial wisdom, as the initiation into destruction and violence, and the negative foundation of philosophy? Here the problem of the absolute foundation (of ungroundedness) reveals its full weight. The fact that man, the animal possessing language, is, as such, ungrounded, the fact that he has no foundation except in his own action (in his own "violence"), is such an ancient truth that it constitutes the basis for the oldest religious practice of humanity: sacrifice. However one interprets the sacrificial function, the essential thing is that in every case, the action of the human community is grounded only in another action; or, as etymology shows, that every* facere *is* sacrum facere. *At the center of the sacrifice is simply a determinate* action *that, as such, is separated and marked by exclusion; in this way it becomes* sacer *and is invested with a series of prohibitions and ritual prescriptives. Forbidden action, marked by sacredness, is not, however, simply excluded; rather it is now only accessible for certain people and according to determinate rules. In this way, it furnishes society and its ungrounded legislation with the fiction of a beginning: that which is excluded from the community is, in reality, that on which the entire life of the community is founded, and it is assumed by the society as an immemorial, and yet memorable, past. Every beginning is, in truth, an initiation, every* conditum *is an* abs-conditum.

Thus the sacred is necessarily an ambiguous and circular concept. (In Latin sacer *means vile, ignominious, and also august, reserved for the gods; both the law and he who violates it are sacred:* qui legem violavit, sacer esto.*) He who has violated the law, in particular by homicide, is excluded from the community, exiled, and abandoned to himself, so that killing him would not be a crime:* homo sacer is est quem populus iudicavit ob maleficium; neque fas est eum immolari, sed qui occidit paricidi non damnatur.

The ungroundedness of all human praxis is hidden here in the fact that an action (a sacrum facere*) is abandoned to itself and thus becomes the foundation for all legal behavior; the action is that which, remaining unspeakable (*arreton*) and intransmissible in every action and in all human language, destines man to community and to tradition.*

The fact that, in sacrifice as we know it, this action is generally a murder, and that sacrifice is violent, *is certainly not casual or insignificant; and yet in itself this violence explains nothing; rather, it requires an explanation (as has been offered recently by Meuli and Burkert [Burkert 1972, English ed. 1983], who place sacrifice in relation to the hunting rites of prehistoric peoples, that is, to the development of hunters from a race of beings that were not biologically destined for hunting). Violence is not something like an originary biological fact that man is forced to assume and regulate in his own praxis through sacrificial institution; rather it is the very ungroundedness of human action (which the sacrificial mythogeme hopes to cure) that constitutes the violent character (that is* contra naturam, *according to the Latin meaning of the word) of sacrifice. All human action, inasmuch as it is not naturally grounded but must construct its own foundation, is, according to the sacrificial mythogeme, violent. And it is this* sacred *violence that sacrifice presupposes in order to repeat it and regulate it within its own structure.*

The unnaturalness of human violence—without common measure with respect to natural violence—is a historical product of man, and as such it is implicit in the very conception of the relation between nature and culture, between living being and logos, where man grounds his own humanity. The foundation of violence is the violence of the foundation. *(In a chapter from* Science of Logic, *titled "The Absolute Relation," Hegel articulates this implication of violence in the very mechanism of every human action as* causative *action; Hegel 3, pp. 233-40.)*

Even philosophy, through the mythogeme of the Voice, thinks the ungroundedness of man. Philosophy is precisely the foundation of man as human being (that is, as a living being that has logos*) and the attempt to absolve man of his ungroundedness and of the unspeakability of the sacrificial mystery. But precisely in that this absolution is conceived on the basis of a having-been and a negative foundation, the liberation of the sacrificial mythogeme remains necessarily incomplete, and philosophy finds itself obliged to "justify" violence. The* arreton, *the unspeakable tradition, continues to dominate the tradition of philosophy: in Hegel, as that nothingness that we must abandon to the violence of history and of language in order to tear away from it the appearance of a beginning and immediacy; and in Heidegger, as the unnamed that remains unsaid in all speech and in all tradition, and destines man to tradition and language. Certainly, in both cases, the aim of philosophy is to absolve man from the violence of the foundation; but this absolution is possible only* at the end *or in a form that remains, at least partially, excluded from articulation.*

A completed foundation of humanity in itself should, however, signify the definitive elimination of the sacrificial mythogeme and of the ideas of nature and culture, of the unspeakable and the speakable, which are grounded in it. In fact, even the sacralization of life derives from sacrifice: from this point of view it simply abandons the naked natural life to its own violence and its own unspeakableness, in order to ground in them every cultural rule and all language. The ethos, *humanity's own, is not something unspeakable or* sacer *that must remain unsaid in all praxis and human speech. Neither is it nothingness, whose nullity serves as the basis for the arbitrariness and violence of social action. Rather, it is social praxis itself, human speech itself, which have become transparent to themselves.*

Epilogue
To Giorgio Caproni

What remains in suspense, what dangles in thought? We can only think, in language, because language is and yet is not our voice. There is a certain suspense, an unresolved question, in language: whether or not it is our voice, as baying is the voice of the ass or chirping the voice of the cricket. So when we speak we cannot do away with thought or hold our words in suspense. Thought is the suspension of the voice in language.

(The cricket, clearly, cannot think in its chirping.)

When we walk through the woods at night, with every step we hear the rustle of invisible animals among the bushes flanking our path. Perhaps they are lizards or hedgehogs, thrushes or snakes. So it is when we think: the path of words that we follow is of no importance. What matters is the indistinct patter that we sometimes hear moving to the side, the sound of an animal in flight or something that is suddenly aroused by the sound of our steps.

The animal in flight that we seem to hear rustling away in our words is—we are told—our own voice. We think—we hold our words in suspense and we are ourselves suspended in language—because, finally, we hope to find our voice in language. Long ago—we are told—our voice was inscribed in language. The search for this voice in language is thought.

The fact that language surprises us and always anticipates voice, that the suspension of the voice in language never terminates: this constitutes the *problem of philosophy. (How each of us* resolves *this suspension is ethics.)*

But the voice, the human voice, does not exist. We have no voice to trace through language, to seize—in order to remember it—at the point where it dis-

*appears in names, where it is inscribed in letters. We speak with the voice we lack, which has never been written (*agrapta nomima, Antigone, *454). And Language is always "a dead letter."*

We can only think if language is not our voice, only if we reach our own aphonia at its very bottom (but in reality there is no bottom). What we call world is this abyss.

Logic demonstrates that language is not my voice. The voice—it says—once was, but is no more nor can it ever be again. Language takes place in the non-place of the voice. This means that thought must think nothing *in the voice. This is its piety.*

Thus the flight, the suspension of the voice in language, must come to an end. We can cease to hold language, the voice, in suspense. If the voice has never been, if thought is thought in the voice, it no longer has anything *to think. Once completed, thought has no more thought.*

Only a trace of the Latin term cogitare, *for centuries a key term indicating thought, remains in the word* intractable *(Italian* tracotanza*). As late as the fifteenth century* coto *and* cuitanza *meant thought.* Intractable *derives from the Latin* ultracogitare, *and passes through the Provençal* ultracuidansa: *to exceed, to pass the limit of thought, to think beyond,* to over-think.

We can repeat that which has been said. But that which has been thought can never be said again. You take your leave forever of the word once it has been thought.

We walk through the woods: suddenly we hear the flapping of wings or the wind in the grass. A pheasant lifts off and then disappears instantly among the trees, a porcupine buries in the thick underbrush, the dry leaves crackle as a snake slithers away. Not the encounter, but this flight of invisible animals is thought. Not, it was not our voice. We came as close as possible to language, we almost brushed against it, held it in suspense: but we never reached our encounter and now we turn back, untroubled, toward home.

So, language is our voice, our language. As you now speak, that is ethics.

Bibliography

Augustine.

De Trinitate, English ed., *The Trinity,* trans. Stephen McKenna, Washington, D.C., 1963.

Benveniste, É.

1. *Problèmes de Linguistique Générale*, vol. 1, Paris, 1966.
2. *Problèmes de Linguistique Générale*, vol. 2, Paris, 1974.

Burkert, W.

Homo Necans, The Anthropology of Ancient Greek Sacrificial Ritual and Myth. Berkeley, 1983. Originally published 1972.

Caproni, G.

Poesie, 1932-1986, Milan, 1989.

Hegel, G. W. F.

1. *Werke in zwanzig Bänden*, vol. 1: *Frühe Schriften*. Frankfurt am Main, 1971.
2. *Werke*, vol. 3: *Phänomenologie des Geistes*. [English ed.: *Hegel's Phenomenology of Spirit*, trans. A. V. Miller, Oxford, 1977.]
3. *Werke*, vol. 6: *Wissenschaft der Logik*, Part 2.
4. *Jenenser Realphilosophie II, Die Vorlesungen von 1805-1806*, ed. J. Hoffmeister, Leipzig, 1931 (2nd ed., *Jenaer Realphilosophie*, Hamburg, 1967).
5. *Jenenser Realphilosophie I, Die Vorlesungen von 1803-1804*, ed. J. Hoffmeister, Leipzig, 1932.
6. *Jenenser Logik Metaphysik und Naturphilosophie*, ed. G. Lasson, Hamburg, 1967 (1st ed., Leipzig, 1923).

Heidegger, M.

1. *Sein und Zeit*, 13th ed., Tübingen, 1972 (1st ed., Halle, 1927). [English ed.: *Being and Time*, trans. John Macquarrie & Edward Robinson, New York, 1962.]
2. *Holzwege*, Frankfurt am Main, 1950. [Partial English ed.: *Poetry, Language, Thought,* trans. Albert Hofstadter, New York, 1971.]
3. *Unterwegs zur Sprache*, Pfullingen, 1967. [English ed.: *On the Way to Language*, trans. Peter D. Hertz, New York, 1971.]

4. *Lettre à Monsieur Beaufret* in *Lettre sur l'humanisme*, German text translated and presented by R. Munier, Paris, 1964.
5. *Wegmarken*, Frankfurt am Main, 1967. [English ed.: *Existence and Being*, trans. R. F. C. Hull, London, 1949.]
6. *Zur Sache des Denkens*, Tübingen, 1969. [English ed.: *On Time and Being*, trans. Joan Stambaugh, New York, 1972.]

Jakobson, R.

"Shifters, verbal categories and the Russian verb," in *Selected Writings*, vol. 2, The Hague, 1971.

Klee, P.

Gedichte, ed. Felix Klee, Zurich, 1960, 1980.

Kojève, A.

1. *Kant*, Paris, 1973.
2. *Introduction à la lecture de Hegel*, ed. R. Queneau, Paris, 1979 (1st ed., Paris, 1947).

Leopardi, G.

Giacomo Leopardi, trans. Jean-Pierre Barricelli, Boston, 1986.

Lohmann, J.

"M. Heideggers Ontologische Differenz und die Sprache," in *Lexis* 1 (1948), pp. 49-106.

Lévinas, E.

Autrement qu'être ou au-delà de l'essence, La Haye, 1978.

Thurot, C.

Extraits de divers manuscrits latins pour servir à l'histoire des doctrines grammaticales au Moyen-Age, in *Notices et Extraits des Manuscrits de la Bibliothèque Nationale, etc.*, vol. 22, Paris, 1874.

Index
Compiled by Karen Pinkus

Theory and History of Literature

Volume 47. Eugene Vance *From Topic to Tale: Logic and Narrativity in the Middle Ages*
Volume 46. Jean-François Lyotard *The Differend: Phases in Dispute*
Volume 45. Manfred Frank *What Is Neostructuralism?*
Volume 44. Daniel Cottom *Social Figures: George Eliot, Social History, and Literary Representation*
Volume 43. Michael Nerlich *The Ideology of Adventure, Volume 2*
Volume 42. Michael Nerlich *The Ideology of Adventure, Volume 1*
Volume 41. Denis Hollier *The College of Sociology (1937-39)*
Volume 40. Peter Sloterdijk *Critique of Cynical Reason*
Volume 39. Géza von Molnár *Romantic Vision, Ethical Context: Novalis and Artistic Autonomy*
Volume 38. Algirdas Julien Greimas *On Meaning: Selected Writings in Semiotic Theory*
Volume 37. Nicolas Abraham and Maria Torok *The Wolf Man's Magic Word: A Cryptonymy*
Volume 36. Alice Yeager Kaplan *Reproductions of Banality: Fascism, Literature, and French Intellectual Life*
Volume 35. Denis Hollier *The Politics of Prose: Essay on Sartre*
Volume 34. Geoffrey Hartman *The Unremarkable Wordsworth*
Volume 33. Paul de Man *The Resistance to Theory*
Volume 32. Djelal Kadir *Questing Fictions: Latin America's Family Romance*
Volume 31. Samuel Weber *Institution and Interpretation*
Volume 30. Gilles Deleuze and Flix Guattari *Kafka: Toward a Minor Literature*
Volume 29. Peter Szondi *Theory of the Modern Drama*
Volume 28. Edited by Jonathan Arac *Postmodernism and Politics*
Volume 27. Stephen Melville *Philosophy Beside Itself: On Deconstruction and Modernism*
Volume 26. Andrzej Warminski *Readings in Interpretation: Hölderlin, Hegel, Heidegger*
Volume 25. José Antonio Maravall *Culture of the Baroque: Analysis of a Historical Structure*
Volume 24. Hélène Cixous and Catherine Clément *The Newly Born Woman*
Volume 23. Klaus Theweleit *Male Fantasies, 2. Male Bodies: Psychoanalyzing the White Terror*
Volume 22. Klaus Theweleit *Male Fantasies, 1. Women, Floods, Bodies, History*
Volume 21. Malek Alloula *The Colonial Harem*
Volume 20. Jean-François Lyotard and Jean-Loup Thébaud *Just Gaming*

Volume 19. Jay Caplan *Framed Narratives: Diderot's Genealogy of the Beholder*
Volume 18. Thomas G. Pavel *The Poetics of Plot: The Case of English Renaissance Drama*
Volume 17. Michel de Certeau *Heterologies: Discourse on the Other*
Volume 16. Jacques Attali *Noise: The Political Economy of Music*
Volume 15. Peter Szondi *On Textual Understanding and Other Essays*
Volume 14. Georges Bataille *Visions of Excess: Selected Writings, 1927-1939*
Volume 13. Tzvetan Todorov *Mikhail Bakhtin: The Dialogical Principle*
Volume 12. Ross Chambers *Story and Situation: Narrative Seduction and the Power of Fiction*
Volume 11. Edited by John Fekete *The Structural Allegory: Reconstructive Encounters with the New French Thought*
Volume 10. Jean-François Lyotard *The Postmodern Condition: A Report on Knowledge*
Volume 9. Erich Auerbach *Scenes from the Drama of European Literature*
Volume 8. Mikhail Bakhtin *Problems of Dostoevsky's Poetics*
Volume 7. Paul de Man *Blindness and Insight: Essays in the Rhetoric of Contemporary Criticism 2nd ed., rev.*
Volume 6. Edited by Jonathan Arac, Wlad Godzich, and Wallace Martin *The Yale Critics: Deconstruction in America*
Volume 5. Vladimir Propp *Theory and History of Folklore*
Volume 4. Peter Brüger *Theory of the Avant-Garde*
Volume 2. Hans Robert Jauss *Toward an Aesthetic of Reception*
Volume 1. Tzvetan Todorov *Introduction to Poetics*

About the Author

Giorgio Agamben is currently director of the philosophy program at the Collège International de Philosophie in Paris and professor of philosophy at the University of Macerata (Italy). In 1966 and 1968, he attended Martin Heidegger's seminars in Le Thor. Since 1982, he has been editor of the Italian edition of Walter Benjamin's complete works. Among other books, he has published *Stanze: La paróla e il fantasma nelle cultura occidentale* (1977); *Infanzia e storia* (1978); *Idea della prosa* (1985); and *Le comunità che viene* (1990).

About the Translators

Karen E. Pinkus is assistant professor of Italian at Northwestern University. She is the author of several articles on visual perception, Jacques Lacan, and ethics.

Michael Hardt recently received his Ph.D. in comparative literature from the University of Washington and expects to receive another doctorate in political theory from the University of Paris (VIII) at Saint-Denis. He is the translator of Antonio Negri, *The Savage Anomaly: The Power of Spinoza's Metaphysics and Politics* (Minnesota, 1991).